The Way We Think:
Chinese
View of Life
Philosophy

中国人的生活哲学

李 钢/编 著

韩清月 周晓刚 张文婷 付志斌 冷 健/翻 译

华语教学出版社
SINOLINGUA

First Edition 2009
Second Printing 2010

ISBN 978-7-80200-411-5
Copyright 2009 by Sinolingua
Published by Sinolingua
24 Baiwanzhuang Road, Beijing 100037, China
Tel: (86) 10-68320585
Fax: (86) 10-68326333
http:// www.sinolingua.com.cn
E-mail: hyjx@sinolingua.com.cn
Printed by Beijing Foreign Languages Printing House

Printed in the People's Republic of China

前　言

　　作为一个关注、爱好"中西文化比较研究"的学者，我多年来读了不少这方面的书，也发表了各种各样这方面的文章和著作，但是它们大都属于时下所谓"曲高和寡，受众较少"的学术文字。

　　几年前有机会到英国剑桥大学读书学习，异域文化环境使我对原先停留于脑海中和纸面上的西方文化有了更多切身感受，也迫使我就过去所读所想的内容进行重新思考。同时，在国外生活时，我也受到了中西文化差异的无数次撞击，对"纸上得来终觉浅，事非经过不知难"这句中国古语有了难以忘怀的感悟。于是就产生了一个心愿：什么时候如果能够将自己所见所闻、感触较深的中西文化差异的东西以比较通俗的方式表达出来，接受广大读者的批评和提升就好了。

　　适逢华语教学出版社翟淑蓉编辑约请我写一本主要面向外国朋友，从中西生活、文化差异角度介绍中国文化的著作，于是欣然接受。但是等到落笔时，才知道自己在做一件根本"力不能及"的事。因为一方面，如果从生活中总结概括中国人"为人处事、接人待物"的特点，总感到左右为难，总觉得会以偏概全，顾此失彼。生活中并不存在传统的或现代的"标准意义"上的中国人，他们是活生生的、彼此有差异的、可能充满矛盾的人，要想从文化上把握中国人的性格、特点，必然面临时空上的困难。传统社会中的中国人总的来讲具有稳定性，或者说比较规范成型，但是我们需要向外国朋友展示的更多的是今天的中国和中国人。而近几十年是中国社会大变革的时代，改革开放、除旧布新给全社会带来了翻天覆地的巨大变化。一个变动中的社会和民众既保留了几千年传统社会的文化习俗，又呈现出在当今全球化时代与世界日益接轨后所带有的新思想和新风貌。权衡再三，我最终选择将"矛盾的状况"展现给读者，唯有这样，才可以更真实地反映这个时代的中国人。知此特殊性，相信中外读者朋友就不会为理解书中的"矛盾"感到"无所适从"了。

全文分为处世篇、家庭篇和德行篇三个部分，从不同角度和场景介绍了三十多个中国人接人待物的处世哲学，尽可能借案例叙事，通俗易懂地昭示或彰显博大精深、纷繁复杂的中国文化。读者可以"借一斑而窥全豹"，以此透视中国人的性格、价值观念和伦理准则。

另外，任何民族的文化都汇集了从不同角度上看可以进行不同价值评价的东西，中国的大众文化也不例外。正如一位哲人所言：一个能够正视自己缺点和不足的民族才是有希望的民族。我正是出于此目的，想通过此书让更多的中外朋友都能从中华文化中了解我们民族的特点，看到我们民族的不懈努力和我们的追求。

最终杀青的文稿虽经反复斟酌修改，自己仍觉得与想达到的境界有不少差距。希望此稿能够树立一个可供读者朋友帮助和批评的靶子，为我今后更好地完成这一有意义的任务奠定基础。

李　钢

2008 年 10 月于北京寓所

Preface

As a scholar who is fond of and cares much about the "Comparative Study of Eastern and Western Cultures", I have read many books in this field over the years and also published various relevant articles and writings. Yet most of them were academic works of the time that were in a way so highbrow that few people could enjoy or understand them.

A few years ago I got a chance to study at Cambridge University in England and it was the cultural environment there that brought me the first-hand understanding of Western culture which previously had been extrapolations from various media sources. I was also compelled to rethink the things that I had read and thought about in the past. Meanwhile, I was stunned several times by the differences between the two cultures during my stay there, providing me an indelible impression of the old Chinese saying: "It is far from enough to dwell upon theory. One will never realize how hard the task is until he has done it himself". I then had a wish: It would be wonderful if I could convey what I have seen and heard about the differences between Eastern and Western cultures that have touched me so deeply in a common and simple manner for the criticism and improvement of the readers.

It so happened that Madam Zhai Shurong, editor of Sinolingua, encouraged me to write a book that might introduce Chinese culture from the perspective of the differences with respect to life and culture between the east and west. I eagerly accepted. But hardly did I realize the monumental task that lay ahead. On one hand, I found myself in an awkward position, unable to include everything at one time and generalize from the lives of Chinese people the characteristics of conducting themselves. There are no "standardized" Chinese people in real life, traditional or modern. But rather, Chinese are people who are diverse if not paradoxical. Moreover, I had to cope with the difficulty regarding space and time when illustrating the personality traits of the Chinese from the cultural angle. Chinese people in the traditional society are generally characterized by their consistency, or in other words, they have already taken certain shape. But what we need to demonstrate to our foreign friends should be more of today's China and its people. The Chinese society has been undergoing a period of massive transformation during recent decades. The policy of reform and opening-up, the undertaking of demolishing the old and establishing the new have brought remarkable changes to the society as a whole. The society and people that are in the middle of these changes may both retain the cultural customs of the tradition-al society which has endured for several thousand years and at the same time take on new thoughts and features that have been brought about by the increasing integration with the rest of the world during this era of globalization. Upon mature consideration, I decided in the end to present readers with "paradoxical situations" as only in this way could I describe the Chinese people of the time in a truthful manner. In light of this peculiarity, I believe readers from China and abroad will no longer be confused when they try to understand the seemingly contradictory points in the book.

The work is divided into three parts, namely, social be-havior, family and moral principles, which introduces over 20 ways Chinese people conduct themselves in society, try-ing to recount things through cases and display the profound and intricate Chinese culture in a way that is easy to under-stand. The readers thus can conjure up the whole through a rather small part so as to get a clear view of the character, values and ethical standards of the Chinese people.

Additionally, the culture of each and every nation may have aspects that can be assessed differently from various angles. The popular culture of China is no exception. A philosopher once said: "Only when a nation acknowledges its own shortcomings can it be promising." For this purpose, I would like to contribute this book to all friends from China and abroad and enable them to understand the characteristics of the Chinese nation through its culture, and see our relentless efforts and pursuit.

Although the final draft has been deliberated and revised time and again, I still feel that it falls short of the ideal level. Hopefully it can serve as a target which will receive the help and criticism of our readers and lay a solid foundation for me to better accomplish this meaningful task in the future.

Li Gang

October 2008, Beijing

目 录
Contents

处事篇
Social Behavior

家庭篇
Family

德行篇
Moral Principles

XI

Contents
目录

处事篇

Social Behavior

1. 面子第一

"面子"是汉语中一个重要而有趣的词，它由字面意思衍生为"尊严"的代名词，并把"尊严"的含义扩大了。"面子"成为渗透于整个中国人社会生活中的一种重要观念。中国人总想在别人面前表现出某种程度的体面和优越感，能够做到这一点就算是有"面子"，反之则是"丢面子"。

中国现代著名文学家鲁迅先生曾经说过，"面子是中国人的精神纲领，只要抓住这个……全身都跟着走动了。"现代国学大师林语堂先生也有过精辟的论述："中国民族的特征之一，就是重人情、重面子。"在中国人看来，"不给面子是最大的无礼"，就如同西方人向对手挑战一样。给人面子，或者要求别人给自己面子，是合乎中国传统文化"礼"的规范的，这乃是中国社会交换的"人情法则"。

对此，许多外国学者也有敏锐的觉察。美国人阿瑟·亨德森·史密斯写的《中国人气质》一书的第一章就叫"给面子"。他发表了自己的看法："在中国，面子这个词，实际上是一个复杂的集合名词，其中包含的意义，比我们所能描述或者可能领悟的含义还要多，

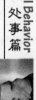

面子问题正是打开中国人许多最重要特性这把暗锁的钥匙。"

面子是构成中国人际关系结构的一个重要因素，而且中国人的面子观念极强，"士可杀，不可辱"，这六个字从古至今教导着许多人。尊严即面子，是一种不可抑止的人生追求。人为自己的尊严发起保卫战时，是连性命都可以丢的，其他的各种努力更不在话下了。

中国秦朝末年著名将领项羽的乌江自刎就是个典型的例子。他打了败仗后退到乌江，本来他是可以乘渔船逃回江东的，但他放弃了，因为他觉得"无颜见江东父老（没有脸回去面对他的乡亲父老）"，最后他选择了自刎。他的死成全了他的尊严，成全了一代枭雄的气节，成就了他名垂青史。可见面子对中国人而言，有时甚至比生命还重要。

历史上还有因伤及面子而差点亡国的教训。据《东周列国志》载：春秋战国时诸侯争霸，齐桓公励精图治，使齐国终成春秋五霸之首。传至齐顷公时，国力仍十分雄厚，晋国、鲁国、卫国、曹国等邻国臣服于齐，每年向齐国上贡。有一年四国派大夫一同出使齐国。但巧的是四国的大夫都有残疾：晋国的郤克是个单眼瞎，鲁国的季孙行父是个秃子，卫国的孙良夫是个瘸子，曹国的公子首是个驼背。齐顷公为讨母亲欢心，便成心想取笑他们。于是他暗中选来眇者、秃者、跛者、驼者各一人，让他们分别服侍四国的使者，这惹得太后和宫女哈哈大笑。四国使者感到丢尽了面子，勃然大怒，于是共商出兵伐齐。三年后，四国结成同盟，大举进攻齐国，齐国大败，从此以后就一蹶不振了。这正是不顾及他人面子而导致的恶果。

事物往往具有两面性。有时强调"面子"是为了国格、人格和尊严，值得人人为之而努力；可有时过于偏狭，为暂时的面子而失去长久的面子也会令中国人吃些苦头，结果导致"死要面子活受罪"。清朝时，中国的农耕文明发展到很高的水平，因而政府自认为天朝物丰，国土辽阔，强大无比，于是不屑与落后的国家交往，采取闭关锁国之策。结果错过了近代人类文明发展的大好机遇，给中国社会的发展和进步带来极大危害。

"好面子"是中国文化中的一个突出现象。由于建立和维持良好的人际关系对个体生存和发展非常重要，因此中国人在交往中很重视他人的看法和感受。

面子之于中国人，是一门处世学问，一门艺术。面子是有大小的。这不是说人的脸有大有小，而是说对于不同的人，面子的影响程度不一样。一般来说，面子的大小和人的社会地位的高低是成正比的。地位越高，官职越大，面子也就越大；反之，地位越低，面子就越小。

当然，老百姓也爱面子，也有自己的尊严。要想与中国人愉快交往，最大的窍门就是给他们留足"面子"，尊重他们的人格和文化习惯。

Mianzi Outweighs All Else

"*Mianzi*" is an important and interesting word in Mandarin Chinese which has evolved into a synonym for "dignity" and even beyond that from its literal meaning. It embodies a significant concept deeply rooted in Chinese society. When with others, Chinese people always take to heart their dignity and superiority, which they hope will earn them due respect. Otherwise, they will "lose face".

Lu Xun, a renowned modern Chinese writer, says that *mianzi* is the key moral to the Chinese. It's like the pigtail everyone wore during the Manchu reign. Once seized by his pigtail, one could not move a single step, but was completely under another's control. In the words of Lin Yutang, a master of Chinese culture, one characteristic of the Chinese nation is their value of humanity and the respect of others. No humiliation would be more unbearable than a wound to their feelings. This is the same as in a duel between two Western gentlemen. To show due respect for others and expect others to do the same in return is the Chinese ritual and rule of exchange in worldly affairs.

Of Chinese *mianzi*, Western scholars also have incisive observations. In *Chinese Characteristics*, Arthur Henderson Smith (1845-1932) talks about *mianzi* in the first chapter. "In China, *mianzi* is an intricate collective noun, which has far more connotations than what we can describe or understand," he writes. "It is the key to discover many important characteristics of the Chinese nation."

Mianzi is an important link in the Chinese social network. Dignity or face is an irresistible pursuit for the face-conscious Chinese. As the old saying goes, a scholar would rather die than be humiliated. To defend his dignity, one would lay down his life, let alone any other efforts.

Xiang Yu, an ambitious general of the Qin Dynasty (221-206 BC), provides one example. After a vital defeat, he could have taken a boat, and fled to his hometown east of the Wujiang River. But, feeling ashamed to face his country folk, he committed suicide. His death saved his dignity and made him revered in history. This shows that to the Chinese, face weighs far more than life.

Humiliation could even incur warfare. As recorded in

Social Behavior
处事篇

Romance of the States of Eastern Zhou, Duke Huan of Qi, a state during the Spring and Autumn Period (770-476 BC), ran his state very well and made it one of the five powers of his time. During the reign of his grandson Duke Qing, Qi was still very powerful, and the neighboring states of Jin, Lu, Wei and Cao all paid tributes to Qi every year. Once, the four states each dispatched an envoy to Qi. Coincidentally, each of the four envoys had some physical disability or undesirable distinguishing characteristic: Xi Ke of Jin had one blind eye, Jisun Xingfu of Lu was bald, Sun Liangfu of Wei was a cripple, and Gongzi Shou of Cao had a hump. To make fun of them and amuse his mother, Duke Qing selected four servants for them: a blind man for Xi Ke, a bald man for Jisun Xingfu, a lame man for Sun Liangfu, and a humpbacked man for Gongzi Shou. The trick entertained the dowager and the court maids, but hurt the four envoys deeply. In private, they agreed on a punitive expedition against Qi. Three years later, the allied force of the four states defeated Qi, which never recovered. This tells how dreadful it could be to disregard others.

Things always have two sides. In some cases, valuing face means to safeguard personal or national dignity and therefore deserves every effort. But in other cases, narrow-minded efforts for face's sake may lead to untold sufferings. In the Qing Dynasty (1644-1911), the Chinese farming civilization had reached a fairly high level. Arrogantly confident in the country's power, abundant resources and vast territory, the Qing court despised any idea of exchange with others and followed a closed-door policy. That decision resulted in China missing great opportunities in modern history for social progress.

Face-consciousness is a typical phenomenon in the Chinese culture. Since establishing and maintaining a favorable social relationship means a great deal to individual development, the Chinese are quite careful about others' opinions and feelings.

To the Chinese, *mianzi* signifies an art of social communication. One's face may be big or small, but his *mianzi* is determined by his social status. Generally, the higher the status and rank he has, the more respect he receives. Of course, common people also care very much about *mianzi* and have dignity of their own. It is highly advisable to give them plenty of "*mianzi*" and recpect their dignity and cultural tradition.

2. 朋友之间喜欢称兄道弟

中国社会中有一种特殊的伦理关系，即"友道"。它是从儒家的兄弟观念延伸到社会的一种亲密纽带。友道不同于血缘关系，也不同于姻亲，社会地位、文化背景和年龄不同的人都可以变成朋友，而最好的朋友完全可以像亲兄弟一样披肝沥胆，有福同享，有难同当。中国人有句古话：在家靠父母，出外靠朋友。一个人成年之后就要离家闯天下，这时起决定作用的就是朋友。

中国人认为兄弟如手足，所以兄弟情常被中国人称为手足情，而且朋友之间也喜欢称兄道弟。中国伦理的核心讲究忠、孝、悌、信、义。"悌"，即兄弟之间友善的、不弃不离的、订之于终生的亲情。在中国人心中，兄弟情是大事。它仅次于忠君报国、侍奉父母，是做人之根本。

中国是一个重"人情"的社会，在中国人的观念中，始终把亲族关系置于人际关系的第一位。在中国人的日常生活中，一位带着孩子的家长，见到同事、邻居时，一般都会教自己的孩子叫"叔叔、阿姨"。对年龄、辈分较长的叫"奶奶、爷爷"。孩子遇到玩伴，父母要指点孩子以兄弟姐妹相称。将社会角色转换成了亲属关系家庭角色是中国社会的一大特色。这是因为相对于西方的个体本位主义而言，中国人所认同的自我是一种更为集体主义的自我。亲属关系的认同构成了中国人际关系的核心，成为最基本的关系认同。以此为核心，中国人会根据目的和需要的不同调整关系认同的标准，例如从亲属关系放宽到准亲属关系、地缘关系乃至业缘关系。关系认同范围的扩展意味着中国人可能将更多的非亲属关系者及其资源吸纳到支持其实现某种目标和需要的行动中来。

　　儒家主张，自我需要的实现有赖他人的支持。新儒学的代表杜维明指出："人们必须注意这一点，儒教的自我发展概念承认人的意志是薄弱的和人是容易犯错误的。假如没有社会经验的支持，一个人单独追求自我的发展是很难想象的事；因此，人要发展必须要尽可能地寻找各种关系的支持。"自我与他人（具有亲属关系之人）的关系是相互的：自我有责任秉承和实现他人的期待；同样，他人也有责任或义务对自我给予支持。

　　在中国古代的四大名著之一《三国演义》里，刘备、关羽、张飞在桃园结义，共同盟誓：不求同年同月同日生，只愿同年同月同日死。三人的手足之情，任凭曹操黄金美女若干，都不能从中觅到空隙离间。此等兄弟情深，

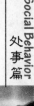

已成为中国后人评述兄弟之情的典范。他们为什么要建立一种这样的关系呢？因为他们认为，只有建立这种兄弟关系，才能找到一种比一般朋友关系更可靠的纽带，而只有这种纽带才是可信任的，可以肝胆相照，共图大事。这在中国历朝历代的封建官僚和他们的从属幕僚之间非常普遍，到处可见称兄道弟的朋友或结义的兄弟关系。

这一现象延至今日，早已融入了中国人的血液中。无论在大小宴会上还是在街头巷尾，称兄道弟的情景随处可见。同处一寝室的大学生总要排个老大、老二……即使毕业多年，他们仍以此相称，感情笃实。如此做法并不是他们看重座次，而是渴望能随时体会到家庭、集体所带给每个人的亲情、手足情。

这种儒家思想中的自我与西方思想中的自我有着很大的差别。在西方，自我是独立的。独立意味着能够为自己的行为负责任，能够减少自己对别人的要求，并且能够对自己的行动加以（内在的）控制。然而，在儒家思想中，自我是依存于他人的。也就是说，自我的发展是需要他人参与的，自我必须秉承他人的期待，这构成了自我对于他人的适应或责任。这种责任意识也是西方个体自我所没有的。

正如 A. J. 马塞勒所比较的，"美国人的自我似乎是通过个人主义来显示其特征的。它倾向于维护个体自我而不是去适应他人，并且为获得高度的自我依赖与独立而奋斗……传统中国人的自我，似乎相对更倾向于有意义的他人而不是倾向于个体自我……无论是西方维护个体的自我还是东方适应他们的自我，都是维持秩序的一种方式而已，不必分什么高下和好坏"。

Brotherly Friendship

There is a unique relationship in Chinese society: brotherly friendship. It is an intimate relationship and an extension of the Confucian concept of brotherhood into social conduct. Friendship differs from blood lineage. People of different social status, cultural background and age can be intimate friends who will go through thick and thin together, just like brothers. There is a Chinese saying: "At home one relies on one's parents and outside on one's friends." It means when one grows up and begins to make a living, his friends will help a lot.

The Chinese believe that brothers are just like hands and feet. So they not only call their friends "brothers", but also treat them as their own brothers. The foundation of Chinese ethics is built on the concepts of loyalty, filial piety, fraternal duty, credit and righteousness. Fraternal duty refers to the lifelong love among brothers. In the heart of the Chinese, brotherly love is next only to loyalty to the motherland and filial piety to the parents. It is an essential part of one's ethical makeup.

The Chinese society values the human side, and always puts the relationship of relatives beyond all other interpersonal relationships. When a father/mother is with the child and runs into a colleague or neighbor, quite often he/she will have the child say hello to them and call them "uncle/aunt" or "grandpa/grandma". When visiting with their pals, the child will be taught to treat them as "brothers and sisters". This is because compared with the egoism of the West, the Chinese endue ego with a more collective meaning. The identification of relationship highlights their understanding of interpersonal communication. People will adjust the criteria for assessing their relationship with others according to their purposes and needs. There may be close relatives, pararelatives, geographical or industrial partners. By expanding the scope of relatives, one can make use of non-relatives and their resources for self-benefit.

The Confucians hold that one has to rely on others to succeed. According to Du Weiming, a contemporary Confucian scholar, the Confucian concept on self-development admits that human will is fragile and humans make mistakes. An inexperienced person can hardly succeed on his own. He must seek help from various connections, and the relationship between people (kindred) is interdependent — one is obliged to fulfill the expectation of others toward oneself. Likewise, others are also obliged to provide support in return.

In *Romance of the Three Kingdoms*, one of China's four classic novels, the three heroes — Liu Bei, Guan Yu and Zhang Fei — swore to be brothers who would rather die together than be divided. Their lasting brotherhood left their rival Cao Cao no chance to destroy their bond, tempting them with gold, beauty or whatever. Why did they choose to build such a brotherly relationship? The answer: Only such a reliable belt could bind them together to share weal and woe. That set a model of bosom brotherhood for the Chinese. Similar relationships were very common among officials and their subordinates throughout feudal Chinese history.

The belief is rooted so deeply in the Chinese society that even today, it's no surprise to see people calling each other "buddy" at banquets or in the streets. Quite often in a college dorm, everyone will be nicknamed "Eldest, Second Eldest..." by their age, just like in an extended family. Even years after graduation, they still use the old address for each other. This is not to stress the seating order, but to engender a sense of being embraced in family love and group attachment.

Such Confucian understanding of ego differs quite a lot from that of Westerners. In the West, an individual is independent, and independence means one is able to take responsibility for his actions, restrain his demand on others, and control his own behaviors. But in the Confucian concept, an individual has to count on others. In other words, self-development involves others, and one must not ignore the expectation of others. So, one must adapt to others and shoulder the responsibilities. Such an awareness of responsibility does not exist in the Western concept of ego.

As American scholar A. J. Massella puts it: "The American ego is featured with individualism, which tends to protect the individuals. Instead of adapting to others, people are encouraged to strive for a high degree of independence and self-reliance.... But the traditional Chinese concept of ego cares more about others, rather than individuals themselves.... Anyhow, both the Western ego of protecting the individuals and that of the East of adapting to others are no more than a way to maintain orders, and there is no need to consider either of them be better than the other."

3. 麻将桌上的做人艺术

在中国，一个人不会因为极聪明就能成功，一个人成功的首要条件不是聪明，而是会做人。打麻将最能体现中国人的这种做人艺术，因而中国人非常适合麻将，麻将也非常适合中国人。

有人说，围棋是聪明人玩儿的游戏，但即便是围棋下得很好的聪明人玩起麻将来，大概也会感到力不从心。有人说打麻将只是靠运气，没有竞技性、对抗性。但中国人的逻辑是：能让最聪明的人也无可奈何的游戏，难道不是最复杂的游戏吗？你不服气，那是你不懂麻将，不懂麻将所代表的中国人的"综合艺术"。外国人用那套归纳演绎和分析的逻辑根本看不懂中国人。

打麻将的时候，人们的心态和表现是形形色色的，细细观察可以看出很多微妙的东西，《红楼梦》《镜花缘》等小说中多有描写。在中国四大名著之一《红楼梦》的第四十七回"呆霸王调情遭苦打，冷郎君惧祸走他乡"中，作者曹雪芹描写了贾母、薛姨妈、王熙凤等人玩儿"碰和牌"，也就是打麻将的情景。其中有这样的情节："鸳

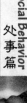

鸯见贾母的牌已十成，只等一张二饼，便递了暗号与凤姐儿。凤姐正该发牌，便故意蹉跎了半晌，笑道，'我这一张牌是在薛姨妈手里扣着呢，我若不发这一张牌，再顶不下来的'。"懂行的人都明白，鸳鸯是在提醒凤姐，赶快讨好卖乖，把手上的那张牌打下来，以便贾母碰和，让老祖宗开心。而凤姐心知肚明，为了不做得太露骨，出牌之前故意表示这是无可奈何。

打麻将欲取得胜利，就必须看住上家、盯住下家、防住对家，而欲出纳得体，进退有据，则须揣度他人手中牌势，知己知彼，上下沟通，左右逢源，瞻前顾后，不似西方扑克牌之两两结对，阵线分明。麻将思维讲究既单打独行，又相互利用，体现出中国传统文化"合而不同"的精神。麻将高手最忌放炮，宁肯自己不和，拆牌苦打，亦万不可将别人可能需要的炮牌打出。

麻将就是这种做人艺术的一个综合反映。在麻将桌上，最重要的不是聪明到能算出多少步，而是根据不同情况灵活适应，采取相应对策，亦即善做人。做人方面的长处在麻将桌上总会得到相应的好处。比如说根据牌型和桌面上已打出的牌制定对策，能成大牌则成大牌，不能成大牌则成小牌，不能成小牌则阻止别人成牌；比如察言观色以判断别人手中的牌。做人的弱点也会带来损失，比如性贪者过于追求大牌反连小牌也成不了；胆小者不敢成大牌只是广种薄收；优柔寡断者因举棋不定而错失良机。这些与其说是一门科学，倒不如说是一门做人艺术，因为道理似乎很简单，但运用起来全要靠机缘和天分了。

说到机缘和天分，这大概是中国人做人方面的两大因素，也是打麻将方面的两大因素吧。机缘其实就是运气，天分就是才干、性格，亦即那种左右逢源的本领和领悟能力。中国人是乐观的，既然决定麻将输赢的因素有两个，也就给了中国人一个选择的空间——赢了是因为技术出色，输了是因为运气不好。就连麻将桌上的常败将军也可以大谈他的"成大牌"经历，自我感觉良好。

西方人的桥牌讲求协作配合，公平竞争。中国人的麻将则要求盯防，各自为政，但在某一方在做极大的牌时，另三家又可暂时联合起来。中国的人际关系在西方人看来简直是一团乱麻，但中国人自有分寸。每个人都有需要的牌在别人手上，每个人手上都有别人需要的牌，乐观的中国人总能在掌握命运的过程中得到乐趣。

麻将让大多数中国人发现了属于自己的天地，属于自己的乐趣，属于自己的人生价值。

Social Behavior
处事篇

Chinese Art of Conduct in Playing Mahjong

In China, one won't succeed by intelligence alone. What determines his success is not his IQ, but his EQ. Playing mahjong best embodies the Chinese art of conduct and it seems that the game was created perfectly for the Chinese.

It's known that the go chess is a game for the clever. But even those who are good at *weiqi* (go) may find difficulty in playing mahjong. Some say mahjong is a game of luck, not of intellectual rivalry. By Chinese logic, isn't the most complicated game the one that can put the brightest people at their wits' end? If using Western logic, you won't understand mahjong, nor the comprehensive art it reflects.

At the mahjong table, few can hide their "tells." A careful observer will find the subtle differences. About this, there is a lot description in Chinese classics such as *Flowers in the Mirror* and *A Dream of Red Mansions*. In Chapter 47 of *A Dream of Red Mansions* titled "A stupid bully is beaten up for his amorous advances, a cool young gentleman leaves home for fear of reprisals", the author Cao Xueqin depicts a game played by Lady Dowager, Aunt Xue, Xifeng and others. "After they had played for a while, Yuanyang noticed that the old lady needed only a 'two of circles' to win the game, and she signaled this to Xifeng whose turn it was to discard. Xifeng deliberately hesitated. 'I'm sure Aunt Xue has the tile I want,' she said, 'If I don't play *this* she'll never part with it.'" When reading this, those familiar with the tricks may know that Yuanyang was nudging Xifeng to discard the very tile so that Lady Dowager would get it and win the round. Of course Xifeng knew that. But to avoid showing her slip, she pretended she had no other choice.

Both being a four-player game, Eastern mahjong and Western bridge have different rules. The latter has two parties allied, while the former has one working on his own and guarding against all three others. To complete the set, one has to figure out what tiles others have and make use of the tiles others discard. The last thing a master-hand wants is to discard the tile another is dreaming of. So quite often, he'd rather lose the set than throw the wrong tile.

This embodies a particular way of conduct. At the game, the most important is not to calculate how far one can go, but to act according to the situation. The strong points in one's personality may serve him well in the game. For instance, by watching the others' mood, one may read their thoughts and guess what tiles they have. A flexible person may change tactics accordingly as the situation changes: trying his best to win the round or at least get the best result possible. Likewise, weak points may lead to disappointment. A greedy person often loses because of his thirst for success; a timid person often yields little despite extensive efforts; an indecisive person often misses the best chance because of hesitation. From this we can see the pastime best reveals the characters of the players. Mahjong is easy to describe, but hard to play, as the game involves both chance and intelligence.

Chance and intelligence are two key factors in social communication. Chance means luck, while intelligence involves talent and personality, or the ability to perceive and get things done one way or another. Since the result is determined by these two factors, it never depresses the optimistic Chinese, as they can easily attribute a win to their good skills and a loss to their poor luck. With such a mindset, a loser always feels comfortable when talking about his past success.

The Western bridge demands fair play and cooperation of two allies, while the Chinese mahjong demands more self-defense. But when one party is nearly going out with a big success, the other three will temporarily join hands against him. Similar examples can be found in personal relationships, which Westerners might view as a total mess. But the Chinese themselves know the network clearly. Everyone has the tile he needs in the hands of others, while holding the tile others need in his own. Such intricacy always delights the optimistic Chinese.

Mahjong is really a game created for the Chinese, to pass time while using their intelligence.

4. "对不起"的不同涵义

细心的外国人可能发现，中国人不像外国人那样在日常生活中经常说"对不起"。外国人会认为中国人不敢承认自己的错误，不肯开口说"对不起"，其实这是不了解中国人。中国人说"对不起"比较少，主要原因在于中国人更注重"慎始"：一开始便考虑会不会造成他人的不便，如果会，就要设法避免，而不是做过了、已经给他人造成了不便才说"对不起"。

中国人的"慎始"观念是让人们时时谨慎，事事小心，不要做"对不起"自己或别人的事情，这样就可以不必说"对不起"。万一防不胜防，出了意外，做出对不起他人的事，也要发自内心地道歉，不可以只随随便便说"对不起"。

明代著名思想家吕坤《呻吟语》中说到"悔前莫如慎始，悔后莫如改图，徒悔无益也"，意思是聪慧、睿智的人，不是没有后悔，而是后悔的机率要小一些，他们往往在重大事情上慎重从事，所以很少后悔。这关键是办事情、处理问题时要三思而后行，尽量考虑周全。如果做过之后还是后悔了，那么不如赶紧想办法来亡羊补牢，光后悔是没用的。以此也可看到中国人的处世原则：说话和做事之前讲究深思熟虑，不能随意说出口或者做出来。因为说错一句话，可能让你受到指责；做错一件事，有可能很久都要为这次过错所牵累。所以懂得为人处世和做事之道的人，在说话和做事时，都会慎言、斟酌，避免自己的言行轻率而引起错误，而不是犯了错误之后说声"对不起"了之。

古代有一句话叫"诸葛一生唯谨慎，吕端大事不糊涂"。赞扬的就是因为谨慎而功成名就的人物。诸葛亮一生无人能及之处便是谨慎。诸葛亮伐魏时布阵于城下，司马懿在城头细细观察良久后抬头与左右众将感叹说："诸葛之才，吾不及也。"于是令紧闭城门，一不许任何人出战，二不许趁夜间偷袭。司马懿此处说的不及之处非进攻之力，而是防守之力。一场战斗最根本之处不在攻，而是守，两军交战，各布战阵，然而先攻的那一方绝对是落于下乘。司马懿看过诸葛亮的布阵，自认无法摆出这等无隙可乘之守势，自不愿出城与之对阵。可见，由于诸葛亮的谨慎避免了一场血战。如果事前考虑不周、鲁莽行事的话，那将会带来多少人员伤亡，连累多少个无辜家庭！那时候说"对不起"没有丝毫意义。

然而，人非圣贤，不可能不犯错。孔子教我们"不二过"，即不要一错再错，"过而能改，善莫大焉"。古人的这番话在今天看来仍具有重要的意义，它告诉我们：做人不要怕犯错误，最重要的是知错就改，并且以后再不犯同样的过失，这才是一个人的可贵之处。

随着中国与世界的不断融合，"对不起"已越来越来深入中国人的心，很多人养成了说"对不起"的习惯。其实在有了小的失误和过错之后，简简单单地说一声"对不起"，就可以赢得对方的理解和宽容，何乐而不为呢？但是，在现实生活中，有的人为了要面子，就是不愿施舍这三个字，结果把问题越闹越大，矛盾越来越激化。

Different Connotations of "Sorry"

Attentive foreigners may find that Chinese people, un-like themselves, do not often say "sorry" in their everyday lives. It is often the case that the Chinese are misunderstood to be fearful of admitting their mistakes and unwilling to say "sorry." The reasons why they seldom say "sorry" are mainly attributed to the environment in which they are brought up in a nation that emphasizes practicality other than form. This requires them to practice *shen shi*, which means thinking from the very start whether to give inconvenience to others. If inconvenience is likely to occur, they would try to prevent it from happening rather than say "sorry" when it is too late.

The concept of *shen shi* of the Chinese is to tell people to be careful with anything at any time and not to do any "regretful" things to themselves or others. Only so can saying "sorry" be avoided. In case of an accident that makes a person regretful for others, an apology should come from his heart and "sorry" not be said casually.

In his *Moaning Words*, Lu Kun, a renowned thinker of the Ming Dynasty (1368-1644), mentioned, "One should do things carefully; otherwise, he regrets afterwards. If he already regrets, he should make corrections in time. It is no good regretting only." In other words, while a wise person may have regrets, his chances of regretting are smaller, because his prudence on major matters leaves no room for regret. The key is to look before you leap when handling things or problems. If a person does something that makes him regret afterwards, he may as well think of a way quickly to make amends. It is of no use to simply express regret.

From this, we can see Chinese principles in dealing with things: one thinks twice, rather than casually, before he speaks or acts. Because for one wrong word you may be blamed; for one wrong act you may be held responsible a long time. Thus, those who know how to deal with people and things are cautious about their words and acts. They mean to avoid mistakes resulting from rashness, rather than merely to say "sorry" to them.

There is an ancient saying to praise two established men of extreme caution in Chinese history, "Zhuge Liang, a military strategist in the Three Kingdoms (220-280), renowned for his lifetime caution, and Lu Duan, Prime Minister in the Northern Song Dynasty (960-1127), for his good sense in handling great matters." Zhuge Liang had no match for his caution. During an attack on a city of the Kingdom of Wei, he commanded a formation in front of Sima Yi, who stood above the city wall. After a careful examination, Sima Yi sighed, "Zhuge Liang is better than me." He then ordered the city gate closed, forbidding anyone to go out seeking a battle with Zhuge Liang, and allowing no surprise attack at night. In terms of the "better" capability Zhuge Liang had, what Sima Yi meant is not in the capability of attacking, but in that of defending. A fundamental factor in battle is not attacking but defending. Two armies fight against each other, with different formations. The first to attack does not necessarily have the upper hand. After analyzing Zhuge Liang's formation and finding no flaw, Sima Yi refused to go out for a battle. Owing to his caution, Zhuge Liang avoided a bloody battle. If you act in a rash way, leading to heavy casualties, including innocent families, saying "sorry" becomes totally meaningless.

However, to err is human. Confucius teaches us not to make the same mistake again. "No good is greater for a person who is aware of his error and able to correct it." This wise saying has great importance even today. A hard-earned merit for a person is not being afraid of making an error, but correcting it when he recognises it and not making similar mistakes in the future.

As China is integrated closer with the world, the word "sorry" has been widely accepted by Chinese people. Many have formed a habit of saying it. In fact, when a small error or mistake occurs, the simplest "sorry" can win understanding and seek forgiveness from others. So why not use it more often? In reality, some who are afraid to lose face are reluctant to say the three words — "I am sorry". As a result, things become worse.

5. 以和为贵

"和"是中国传统文化中极为重要的思想范畴。它虽然具有哲学意味，但立足点仍在于社会的稳定与协调，并直接影响着中国人的思维方式与处世观念。

在中国古代的经典论述中，"和"的基本涵义是和谐。古人重视宇宙自然的和谐、人与自然的和谐，尤其注重人与人之间的和谐。孔子主张"礼之用，和为贵"；孟子提出"天时不如地利，地利不如人和"。"和"既是人际行为的价值尺度，又是人际交往的目标所在。

中国人历来把"和为贵"作为待人处世的基本原则，努力追求着人际之间的和睦、和平与和谐。以诚信、宽厚、仁爱待人是为了"和"；各守本分、互不干涉、"井水不犯河水"是为了"和"；"和而不同"、求同存异、谋求与对立面的和睦共处也是为了"和"。总的看来，"贵和"能有效地避免过激或对抗行为，减少人际摩擦与社会内耗，使中国人的人际关系带有浓重的人情味，从而有利于社会稳定。

自儒家提倡人与人之间应"贵和"以来，人们充分认识和理解了"贵和"的重要性，并把"和为贵"作为"和谐"处世的箴言，常被挂在嘴边。人们在身份和等级不能完全消除的情况下，用亲情、友情、温情相亲相和。

人与自然之间也"贵和"。古代，与松、竹、梅"岁寒三友"相随相伴的，甚至视"梅"为"妻"、将"松"作"子"的大有人在。而在诗文、著画中描述人景和谐相处、构成完美图景的更是数不胜数。如柳永在《望海潮》中写到："重湖叠巘清嘉，有三秋桂子，十里荷花。羌管弄晴，菱歌泛夜，嬉嬉钓叟莲娃。千骑拥高牙。乘醉听箫鼓，吟赏烟霞。异日图将好景，归去凤池夸。"在这里，吹奏乐器的人、随歌声泛舟的人、醉听乐曲的人、吟诗观赏美景的人、在莲叶丛中垂钓的老人和嬉闹的孩童，在十里荷花湖边，伴着秋色美景，享受着安泰祥和的生活，真是一幅令人心驰神往的景色。

明代思想家王廷相在《慎言》中，也多处提到"和"的重要性。如"君臣和则国政和，国政和则民安，故和者治之门也"。这是说，君臣之间的"和"可以带来国家"和"，国家"和"则人民安康，因而，"和"是治国的"门道"。

另外，我们还知道有许多关于"和"的脍炙人口的故事。如"将相和"：武将廉颇傲视没有武功而位居其上的文官蔺相如。当廉颇知道蔺相如是为了国家的利益不跟他计较后，就向蔺相如负荆请罪。强大的秦国见此，也不敢欺侮赵国。再如三国时诸葛亮"南和孙权"，才有了后来"赤壁之战"等的胜利；而关羽拒"和"东吴，不仅失去了荆州，而且最后父子双双死于非命。

故曰：生命和则康，自然和则美，社会和则安，国家和则强。"贵和"不仅利于本人，也利家，更利国。"以和为贵"是一种处世的态度，是一种生命的境界。懂得和谐处世的人是幸福的，快乐的。相反，成天为自己的名利得失斤斤计较、牵肠挂肚、思虑重重的人只会被各种各样没完没了的焦虑和烦恼所困扰，永远也不会享受到人生应有的快乐和生活美好的滋味。

Harmony

"Harmony" is an important category of thought in traditional Chinese culture. Although the concept initially comes from philosophy, it stands for a stable and integrated social life. It directly influences Chinese people's way of thinking and dealing with the world.

In the ancient classic works of China, "harmony" can, in essence, be understood as being harmonious. Ancient people stressed the harmony of the universe and the natural environment, the harmony between humans and nature, and what is more, the harmony between people. Confucius emphasized this when he said that "In the usages of decorum it is harmony that is of value." Mencius advanced this idea when he wrote that "A favorable climate is not as good as topographical advantage, but topographical advantage is not as good as unity and coordination among people." "Harmony" is not only a measure of value, but also the goal of people's associations.

Traditionally Chinese people take the principle as a way of life and try their best to have friendly and harmonious relations. In order to reach "harmony," people treat each other with sincerity, tolerance and love, and do not interfere in other people's business. As the saying goes, "Well water does not intrude into river water", so keeping people's business separate means there will be fewer problems. When people are on good terms but hold different opinions, they should seek common ground and preserve their differences. To seek common ground between two conflicting groups makes for harmonious relations. In sum, to value harmony is to effectively avoid extreme attitudes and confrontational actions and reduce the conflicts between people and the sources of social friction. This is beneficial to Chinese society because

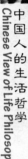
it enriches people's relationships by adding a human touch and promotes stability.

Since Confucians promoted the value of harmony between people, the Chinese people also feel strongly about it and "Harmony is of value" serves as an advisory or caution in their philosophy of life. People find pleasure with each other as relatives, friends, treating each other with affection regardless of differences in social status and class.

There is also the harmony between humans and nature. In ancient times, many scholars identified the "three cold-weather friends" — pine, bamboo and plum, and they even spoke of the "plum blossom" as a wife, and the "pine" as a son. There are countless poems that describe the harmony between humans and nature, all forming perfect images of the relationship. For example, Liu Yong, a Chinese poet of the Song Dynasty wrote in "Look at the Sea Tide": "Clear waves pile up on the lakes, with late autumn Guizi, ten miles of lotus flowers. A Qiang flute plays beautifully, water caltrops sing floating in the evening, an old man fishes and playing children pick lotus flowers. Thousands of cavalrymen escort Gaoya, riding and playing flutes and drums, singing while they admire the mist of evening glow, go back and praise the beauty of ponds." The poem described a place where everyone would want to go: people playing music, boats floating with the songs, people being intoxicated with the music and others reciting poems all in the context of the beautiful ornamental scenery, old men fishing and young children joking around the lotus flowers, people enjoying a carefree life beside the ten-mile-long lake.

In his book *Shen Yan* (*Prudent Words*), Wang Ting-xiang, a Confucian thinker of the Ming Dynasty, often mentions the importance of harmony. One such comment is, "If the monarch and his officials are on good terms, the national affairs will be peaceful. If the nation is peaceful, its people will live a happy life. Therefore, harmony is the way of managing a country."

In addition, we know of many popular stories about harmony. One of them, "Harmony of General and Minister of State" (from *the Records of the Historians*) by Sima Qian (145–? BC) describes the rivalry of two officials who served King Huiwen in the State of Zhao (268–266 BC). The two officials were, Lian Po, a distinguished general, and Lin Xiangru, a prime minister with a rank superior to that of the general. Lian Po resolved to humiliate Lin, but Lin avoided a confrontation. When Lian Po understood that Lin Xiangru put their country's fate before private feuds, he offered

Lin his humble apology. The powerful Qin State saw that this feud was resolved and did not dare to attack the State of Zhao. Yet another example concerns Zhuge Liang, who, to accomplish his famous Longzhong Plan, traveled in person to Eastern Wu and formed an alliance with its ruler, Sun Quan. Hence, he was able to ally the armies of Liu Bei and Sun Quan to defeat Cao Cao in the Battle of Red Cliff in 208. Unfortunately, the union with Sun Quan broke down when the defender of Jingzhou City Guan Yu refused to make peace, so he not only lost the Jingzhou City, but, along with his son, also lost their lives.

From this we learn that a harmonious life is a healthy life; a harmonious nature is a beautiful nature; a harmonious society is a safe society; and a harmonious country is a strong country. The value of harmony is its benefit for the individual, the family and the country. "Harmony is of value" imparts an attitude with which to deal with the world around you and an idea about life itself. People with this attitude should be happy and cheerful. On the contrary, if you are obsessed with narrow personal gain and loss, you will be deeply distressed and anxious; you will feel persecuted by an endless number of worries and can never enjoy or taste the happiness of life.

6. "让" 还是 "不让"

　　中国人是同时说两句话的民族，一方面说"让一步海阔天空"，另一方面则鼓励大家"当仁不让"。到底要"让"还是"不让"？答案十分清楚："应该让的时候要让，不应该让的时候，必须不让。"

　　中国传统佛家名篇——《菜根谭》中指出："径路窄处，留一步与人行；滋味浓时，减三分让人尝。此是涉世一极安乐法。"这句话旨在说明谦让的美德。只要心中经常有这种想法，那么人生就会快乐安详。凡事让步，表面上看来是吃亏了，但事实上由此获得的必然比失去的多。

　　一般说来，社交过程中产生矛盾，双方可能都有责任，但作为当事人应该主动地"礼让三分"，多从自己方面找原因。忍让实际上也就是让时间、让事实来表白自己。这样可以摆脱相互之间无原则的纠缠和不必要的争吵。忍让是一种美德。亲人的错怪，朋友的误解，讹传导致的轻言，流言制造的是非……此时生气无助云消雾散，恼怒不会春风化雨，而一时的忍让则能帮助恢复你应有的形象，得到公允的评价和赞美。

清朝时有两家邻居因一道墙的归属问题发生争执，欲打官司。其中一家求助于在京当大官的亲属张英帮忙。张英没有出面干涉这件事，只是给家里写了一封信，力劝家人放弃争执。信中有这样几句话："千里求书为道墙，让他三尺又何妨？万里长城今犹在，谁见当年秦始皇。"家人听从了他的话，邻居也觉得不好意思，两家握手言欢，反而由你死我活的争执变成了真心实意的谦让。

忍让不是懦弱可欺，相反，它更需要的是自信和坚韧的品格。忍让是一种眼光和度量，是雄才大略的表现，能克己忍让的人，是深刻而有力量的。"小不忍则乱大谋"，是指要想成大事必须暂时忍小痛，但绝对不是叫你总是忍，一味地忍让是一种无能的表现。孔子说："当仁，不让于师。"意思是说："只要是行仁义的事，就是在老师面前也不必谦让"。由此可见，凡事让于师是遵从师道尊严，当然不错。但是，只要是行仁义的事，也就不能拘泥了。这里又包含两个方面的意思，一个意思是当自己的意见和老师的意见发生分歧时，老师错了，自己是对的，这时就不必谦让，而应该坚持自己正确的看法。这与古希腊哲学家亚里斯多德那句名言"吾爱吾师，吾更爱真理"不谋而合。另一个意思是只要是行仁义的事，就要自告奋勇，积极主动上前，而不要谦让于其他的人。

既然连老师都不必谦让，其他人自然都不在话下。所以我们今天大都说"当仁不让"而省去"于师"两个字。那意思就是说，只要是行仁义的事，合于仁义，那就什么人都不必让了。

在现实生活中，让，就是放下架子，善于让步和妥协，采取一种"水往低处流"的谦恭态度；不让，就是高高昂起头，维护自己的尊严和权益，表现出一种舍我其谁、当仁不让的气概。能屈能伸，刚柔并济，这在中国是男子汉大丈夫的气度和风范。

To Be Modest or Not

Chinese people advocate two kinds of attitudes regarding modesty, "Take a step back and a boundless world appears before you," and "Feel duty-bound to shoulder a responsibility." Should we or should we not be modest? The answer is this: There are times when modesty is called for, and those when modesty must not be exercised.

Tending the Roots of Wisdom, containing traditional Chinese thoughts of Buddhism, points out the virtue of modesty: On a narrow road, one should stop and wait until

Social Behavior
处事篇

another from the other side to pass first; when having delicious food, one should set aside one third to share with others. This is an excellent way to conduct ourselves in society. If a person always keeps such modesty in mind, his life will be delightful and smooth. Those who seem to always lose actually gain more.

Generally speaking, if there are social conflicts, both parties concerned may be held responsible. Both should take the initiative to show modesty, looking for problems on their own part. To give in first for modest reason is to let time and facts vindicate themselves, so unnecessary quarrels and unscrupulous dealings with the other party can be avoided. Such a modest behavior is a virtue. In cases of misunderstandings arising among relatives and friends, followed by rumors and false comments, anger or fury will not resolve disputes, while temporary toleration can restore a good image, thus gaining fair appraisal and praise.

In the Qing Dynasty, two neighbors had a dispute over the position of a wall dividing their land and were ready to go to court. One of them turned to a powerful relative Zhang Ying, then a high-ranking official in the capital of Beijing. Zhang did not use his influence, but wrote a letter instead, in which he said, "You wrote me for just a narrow piece of land; I would give them a space of three *chi* wide. While the Great Wall remains to this day, the First Emperor of Qin is no more." Zhang's relatives understood the meaning and followed his advice. Their neighbor also felt embarrassed and withdrew three *chi* too. The two neighbors restored their friendship, no longer striving for land but showing heartfelt modesty.

To be modest is not to be cowardly; instead it requires confidence and forbearance. It is considered a kind of insight and generosity. He who can control himself has profundity and strength. It is a manifestation of great talent and broad vision. Little forbearance may breed great mischief. If you want to accomplish a great thing, you must bear small pains, but it is not forbearance without end. If so, it is incompetence.

Confucius said, "In terms of benevolence, there is no need for people to show modesty even before their teacher." Thus, it is not wrong to obey and respect teachers, showing modesty for everything before them. But when practicing justice and benevolence, they should not allow their hands and feet to be tied. This contains two meanings: first, when a person's correct opinion conflicts with his teacher's wrong one, he should not be modest, but insist on his position. Such an interpretation matches Greek philosopher Aristotle's motto, "I love my teacher, but love truth more." Second is to actively practice what is benevolent or just rather than inactively be modest in front of others.

If modesty is not required regarding benevolence, even before one's teachers, there is no need for modesty before others. Today when we talk about practicing benevolence, we omit "in front of teachers." This means that one should not be passive when practicing what is thought be just and benevolent.

42

In real life, being modest means relinquishing one's haughty air, being good at compromise and taking a humble attitude. Not to be modest is to hold high one's head, maintaining dignity and rights, and showing willingness to surpass others. For a great Chinese man, his bearing should be modest, but only when necessary.

7. 饭桌文化

中国古代圣贤说过："民以食为天！"吃饭，不仅是人类生存的第一需要，它还是一种生活方式。吃饭，除了充饥，还包括为什么吃，与什么人同吃，在哪里吃，吃什么，怎样吃。吃在中国早已成为一种文化。

中国人的社交观念很多都和"吃"有关，比如把不熟悉的人叫做"生人"，把相互了解的人叫做"熟人"。不仅如此，生活的种种似乎都可以和"吃"搭上关系：受重视叫"吃香"，混得好叫"吃得开"，嫉妒别人叫"吃醋"，拿佣金叫"吃回扣"，长得漂亮叫"秀色可餐"，觊觎某物叫"垂涎三尺"……中国历史上，"鸿门宴"、"杯酒释兵权"等传奇故事都把饭桌当做解决重大政治、军事、外交问题的最佳场所，"折冲樽俎"更成了不战而屈人之兵、在觥筹交错之间战胜对手的理想境界。"吃"这个词，在中国人的社交生活里被发挥得淋漓尽致。中国人习惯于把饭桌摆在社交的核心地位，使得本来功能单一的饭桌成了纷繁复杂的社会万象的一个缩影。

今天，饭桌文化在中国不仅承载了双方情感的传达，而且发挥着其社交功用。钱钟书就曾著文写道："吃饭有许多社交的功用，譬如联络感情、谈生意经等等。社交的吃饭种类虽然复杂，性质极为简单。把饭给有饭吃的人吃，那是请饭；自己有饭可吃而去吃人家的饭，那是赏面子。交际的微妙不外乎此。"著名出版家沈昌文先生说起和作者打交道的经历时说："我是主张吃的。跟文化人或者思想家要搞好关系，我没别的手段，只有一条——吃。因此到哪里去吃，重要的是我要了解他喜欢吃什么。饮食便于进入主题，就有话可谈了嘛。"

于是中国人谈情说爱请客吃饭，结婚生子请客吃饭，升官晋职请客吃饭，转行跳槽请客吃饭，乔迁新房请客吃饭……另外，老乡会、同学会、生日会吃一顿司空见惯，拿了奖学金、找了好工作，大家统统饭桌上见。

研究饭局文化，就是观察中国几千年来文明史流变的一个窗口。所谓的历史纵横，文化长廊，风土人情，上下五千年，其实都蕴藏于日常生活的吃喝之间。所谓饭局之妙，不在"饭"而尽在"局"也——端的是饭局千古事，得失寸唇知。

具有社交功用的中国式饭局，可以向对方传达"不见外"的信息，代表亲近，即认同对方是"自己人"。饭桌上谈事情比较随意，谈成最好，谈不成就吃饭喝酒，也不伤感情。

在吃饭的具体方式上，中国人的讲究也极多。

在餐桌的安排上，中国人喜欢十人以上的大圆桌胜过小方桌，人多热闹嘛，也更有集体的感觉。在入座的方式上，中国的餐桌有尊卑之分，一般是里面的座位尊，外面靠门的座位卑。在点菜的方式上，西餐馆给每个人一份菜单，各人点各自喜欢的菜，非常简单。中餐馆一般给每桌一个或几个菜单，一桌人共同点菜。每人要尽量选择大家爱吃的菜，不能只顾自己的口味。在用餐方式上，西餐是自己吃自己的，关系较好的，也顶多尝尝对方的菜。中餐的酒桌文化内容丰富多彩得多，落筷的顺序，还有劝酒、劝菜的学问都很大。付账方式，也是颇有学问的。中国人吃饭前大多已经清楚谁买单、谁请客，较少实行 AA 制。因为中国人的交际性聚餐，吃什么不是关键的，关键是吃谁的、跟谁吃、为什么吃，这些问题解决了，付账问题自然迎刃而解。

中国的饮食之道，也是人情融合之道。虽说对此形式有人喜来有人忧，但人们仍是乐此不疲。毕竟它在中国人繁忙的工作之余起到调剂放松的作用。一个简单饭局，既便于亲朋故交之间的沟通交流，也可作为生意对手间的交锋谈判。所谓人脉，所谓圈子，所谓社会关系，所谓资源，所谓一个人的能量，所谓友谊，所谓生意和交易，最后通通绕不开饭局。在吃喝之间联络了感情，解决了难题，化解了矛盾，这也是中国人处事哲学的突出表现。

The Culture of Eating

Ancient Chinese sages have said, "Food is what matters most to people." Eating is the first necessity for human survival. It is also a lifestyle. In addition to allaying one's hunger, eating connotes the following: with whom to eat, where and what to eat, why and how to eat. Eating has long been a culture force in China.

Many Chinese social concepts have connections with eating. For example, a stranger is called *sheng* (uncooked) *ren* (person), and an acquaintance *shu* (cooked) *ren* (person). Besides these, a number of other things in everyday life seem to be associated with eating: being highly appraised and valued is called *chi* (eating) *xiang* (deliciously); getting along well with others is *chi* (eating) *de kai* (*widely*); being jealous is *chi* (eating) *cu* (vinegar); being beautiful is *xiu se ke xian* (beauty can serve as a meal); coveting something is *chui yan san chi* (to have one's saliva drip down three feet long) … In Chinese history, legendary stories, such as *hong men yan* (a dinner party at Hongmen) and *bei jiu shi bing quan* (a cup of wine relieves military power), all have regarded dinner tables as the best occasion to resolve major political, military and diplomatic issues. *Zhe chong* (chariot) *zun zu* (vessels for wine and meat) depicts an ideal state of defeating opponents in a dinner party without using force. Eating has been used thoroughly in Chinese social lives. Chinese place the dinner table at the central point of social contact, making it an epitome of complicated social phenomena.

Today, table culture in China not only conveys mutual feelings but also fulfills the function of social communication. Chinese writer Qian Zhongshu wrote, "Eating performs many social functions, such as, establishing close relationship, or settling a business contract. Though being complicated in various types in society, eating has a simple nature. Offering a meal to a person who can afford his meal is inviting him to a dinner. Going to dine at somebody else's dinner party is to give face. The nuance of social contact lies in examples such as these." A renowned publisher Shen Changwen told of his experience with writers, "I favor eating. To deal with educated people, or get on well with thinkers, dining with them may be my only contact, so where to eat, and most importantly, what he likes to eat, is most important. Eating facilitates topics, and we have things about which to talk."

There are numerous occasions for Chinese people to

come together to eat at the same table: wooing lovers, getting married, giving birth to a son, getting a promotion, quitting one's present job and finding a new one, moving to a new home. More common occasions include being awarded scholarships, finding a good job, and various parties for classmates, townsfolk and birthday celebrations.

Studying table culture can serve as a window to observe Chinese civilization in its thousands of years' evolution. Five thousand years of history, culture and customs are manifested in eating. The excellence of dinner parties does not lie in just "eating," but parties, through which diners may reach their goals.

A Chinese-style dinner party has functions of social contact, sending a message of becoming close friends, and identifying all diners as part of the same group. To talk about business at a dinner table is casual and straightforward for Chinese people. If failing to settle business, the diners can still eat and drink without hurting each other.

In terms of a dinner party, the Chinese pay great attention to detail.

First, when arranging a dinner table, Chinese people love round tables of over ten guests, rather than small square tables. Many diners and a merry atmosphere give a greater sense of togetherness. Second, on the issue of taking seats, respectful and humble seat places are clearly defined for a Chinese table, with the former usually inside and the latter outside by the door. Third, in terms of ordering food in a Western-style restaurant, each diner is given a menu to choose what he likes. In traditional Chinese restaurants one or two menus are generally provided for a table. Diners choose food together, so they try to select food everybody likes, without catering to personal preferences. Fourth, regarding the eating style, each diner in the Western restaurant eats food from his own plate, simplifying the situation. Or he may taste somebody else's food one or two times at most. At a Chinese dinner party, there are plenty of factors: the order of putting down chopsticks, or persuading people to drink more wine or eat more dishes. Finally, with respect to paying for the dinner, there are also many things to learn. Before coming to dinner, the Chinese know much about who should pay or who is treating them to the dinner. They rarely go Dutch. Because Chinese dinners are mostly for social contact, the key is not what to eat, but who should pay the bill, with whom to dine, and why to dine. When all of the above are known, the decision regarding who takes the bill is naturally solved.

Social Behavior
处事篇

50

Chinese dinner parties also contribute to close relationships between people. Though some may like or dislike it, people are still willing to use dinners as a way to build their friendship. For Chinese people, dining together serves as a lubricant in their busy lives. A simple dinner party may serve as a communication point among relatives or friends, or a negotiation between business partners. The so-called human connections, circles, social relations, resources, a person's capability, friendship, or business and transactions can never get round the dinner party in the end. Eating and drinking promotes friendship, and resolves difficulties and conflicts. Cultural dining is also an outstanding Chinese way of dealing with matters.

8. 集体高于个人

　　个人主义价值观与集体主义价值观的差异是东西方文化差异中的一个显著方面。在西方人看来，一切都是为了实现个人的价值和权利而服务的。但是，在中国人看来，集体却是高于一切的。没有集体，哪来的自我？

　　中国几千年的农业文明与儒家思想的深远影响决定了中国的传统价值观是以集体取向为基础的。这里的集体关系，不只包括个人与家庭之间的关系，还包括个人与国家、民族、社会、他人之间的关系。在中国传统的宗法社会里，社会的基本组成单位是家庭而非个人，在这种血缘关系网络中，每个人都十分明确自己的义务、责任。父母、家族养育后代，后代行"孝"回报父母和家族。那时候，个人的命运是与他赖以生存的家庭及家族的命运息息相关的，一损俱损，一荣俱荣。离开了家庭和家族谈个人，就没有任何的实质意义。

　　这种观念现在仍有众多表现。例如旅行，西方人有钱的天马行空，没钱的自助旅行，除非年老行动不便和特殊情况，多数人是不愿意集体旅游的。与西方人总喜

Social Behavior
处事篇

欢独来独往，愿意留给自己足够的个人空间的习惯不同，中国人喜欢热闹，出行、吃饭、穿衣以及工作等等，都讲究大伙儿一起，否则太孤独寂寞。中国人喜欢有人陪伴，不喜欢独处。西方人在独来独往的过程中自得其乐，中国人在热闹相处时得到了同样多的快乐。

中国人既然喜欢一起行动，当然首先是要顾全大局，个人要服从于集体。这是因为中国文化的思想内核是群体意识，而西方文化的思想内核是个体意识。所谓个体意识，就是认为每个人都是单独的个体，是具有独立人格和自由意志的人，因为具有独立人格，每个人的选择和行为，他人都不能强加干涉，大至总统选举，小至职业选择，都如此。所谓群体意识，就是认为个人都是群体的一部分，群体的利益就是个人的利益，群体的价值就是个人的价值。

中国人注重维护群体利益，保障群体团结，实现群体目标。在群体取向的影响下，中国人提倡凡事以社会、集体利益为重，群体的利益大于个人的利益。个人利益应该融入集体利益，必要时可以忽略或牺牲个人利益。群体取向进一步延伸就变成他人取向。

在做事情时，中国人首先考虑别人怎么看、怎么说。人们推崇谦虚知礼，在稳定中求进步、求发展，追求随遇而安，不喜欢争强好胜。同时，社会舆论也往往对过于突出的个人多有微词，正所谓"行高于人，众必非之"，"树大招风"，"枪打出头鸟"。

中国人从小就意识到自己是儿子、女儿，将来还会是丈夫、妻子，父亲、母亲……因而他必须为某一个群体负责，以他们的悲喜为悲喜，以他们的意志为意志。时至今日，如果有人在思想观念、行为举止、甚至服饰装扮上表现出鲜明的个性，也有可能会遭到非议、排挤和厌弃。

儒家文化是一种尚群的文化，它所理解的人是群体之人，而不是具有独立性的个人。杜维明先生指出，儒家的自我是向着他人开放的，离开他人就没有自我；人只有在把自我的需要对象化为他人的需要时，才能获得自我。这就是所谓"己欲立而立人，己欲达而达人"。因此，在儒士眼中，个人与大众的关系犹如水滴与大海的关系，水滴之于大海是渺小和微不足道的，离开大海就会干枯，只有汇入大海，才能获得力量，获得生机。因此，个人应该与大众在思想和行动上整齐划一，步调一致，形成合力。也就是说，中国人的思维方式是注重求同而不是求异。虽然儒家有时也说"和而不同"，也提倡一种特立独行的精神，然而，从总的价值取向上来看，儒学始终坚持的仍然是以群体为本位的道德理念。

因此，中国文化中没有典型个人主义与集体主义的关系和冲突，有的是君子与小人的关系。君子与小人无现实意义上的冲突，有的只是道义上的冲突，即君子与小人的分别。由此，个人主义与集体主义的关系，在中国传统中就变成了君子与小人的关系。古代君子与小人关系的调节机制，是君子理解小人、垂范以感化小人，并期待小人都成为君子，是谓大同。所谓国不以利为利，以义为利也。社会的需求在于培养君子和君子人格，以引导社会向善。

以孔孟为核心的儒家文化为中国人提供了一套独特的人生哲学：个人是沧海一粟，微不足道；众人拾柴火焰高；团结就是力量；"国家兴亡，匹夫有责"。中国历代仁人志士都以"先天下之忧而忧,后天下之乐而乐"、"人生自古谁无死，留取丹心照汗青"、"穷则独善其身，达则兼济天下"为一生追求的最高境界。这些名言佳句不仅成为中华民族代代传承的千古绝唱，而且也充分体现了中国人的价值观念。

The Collective Is Superior to the Individual

One of the outstanding differences between Eastern and Western cultures is the difference in values of individualism versus collectivism. For Westerners, everything serves for the individual's values and rights, while Chinese believe the collective is superior to everything as there could not be a self without the collective.

The traditional value of the Chinese is formed on the basis of a collective orientation, as profoundly influenced by thousands years of agricultural civilization and Confucianism. The collective relationship not only includes the relationship between an individual and his family, but also between the individual and the country, the nation, the society, as well as other individuals. In the traditional patriarchal society of China, the basic components are families, instead of individuals. In the network of blood relationships, each individual is entitled with clear obligations and responsibilities. The parents and the family raise the offspring, and the offspring perform their filial piety towards the parents and the family. The destiny of the individual is intimately linked with that of his family or clan that the individual relies on. When the family is prosperous, so is the individual, and when the family ends up ruined, so does the individual. The individual has little relevance outside the context of family and clan.

Such value is represented in many aspects nowadays. Take traveling as an example. In the West, most people do

Social Behavior

处事篇

not prefer traveling as a group. Whether rich or not, they prefer to be individual travelers with sufficient personal space for themselves. The Chinese are different in that they prefer being together, whether it is traveling, dining out, or working as a team. Or they will feel quite lonely. The Chinese generally love being accompanied and hate being alone. As a matter of fact, the Westerners receive similar pleasure in their independence as the Chinese do when being together.

Since the Chinese love being together, it is paramount to take the interests of the group, or the collective into account, and the individual must follow the will of the collective. The reason behind this is that the philosophical core of Chinese culture is an awareness of the collective, while the philosophical core of the Western culture is an awareness of the individual. The awareness of the individual means that each person is an independent individual with his own personality and will. His choices and behaviors shall not be intervened by any others, might it be a presidential election or a job choice. The awareness of the collective means that the individual is but a part of the collective, and the collective interest is the individual's interest. The collective value is the individual's value.

The Chinese pay more attention to the protection of the

interest of the collective, the solidarity of the collective, and the achievement of the collective goal. They put a heavier weight on the social or collective interest, which is considered more important than individual interest. Individual interest is to be integrated into the interest of the collective, or to be ignored or compromised when necessary. The collective orientation, if further extended in its implication, turns into an orientation or concern of other people.

When doing something, the Chinese tend to consider what others might think or say. Modesty and courtesy are virtues praised highly by the Chinese. Progress and development shall be made in a stable environment. The Chinese prefer to adapt themselves to different circumstances, not to contend for attention or gain. Public opinion is more likely negative towards individuals that stand themselves out. This sentiment is expressed in many Chinese axioms such as: "Detraction pursues the great." or "A tall tree inspires the wind." or "The bird which takes the lead gets shot first."

Starting at young age, Chinese people indentify themselves as the children of their parents. When growing older, they are spouses or parents of other people. They must shoulder certain responsibility for others, follow the emotions of others, or compromise to the will of others. If

one is idiosyncratic in his mind, behavior, or even dress or appearance, he will may be detracted, excluded or rejected.

Confucianism is a culture that encourages the collective. A member of such a culture is not an independent individual but belongs to a collective. Professor Tu Weiming of Harvard University pointed out that the self in the context of Confucianism is relative to the others. There will be no self without other people. And the self will be fulfilled only when what the self's needs are turned into the needs of the others. According to Confucius, "He who wishes to establish himself, seeks also to establish others; wishing to be enlarged himself, he seeks also to enlarge others." So in the eyes of those who believe in Confucianism, the relationship between the individual and the collective is just like that between a drop of water and the sea. A drop of water is trivial and will soon dry up. But if it joins the sea, it gains vitality and power. That said, the individual should think alike and take concerted action with the collective, and should join in the collective for strengthened capability or power. That is to say, the mentality of the Chinese is to seek what's in common and to set aside what's different. Though Confucianism sometimes suggests "keeping the differences but still being in harmony", and encourages individualistic spirit. But on the whole, Confucianism has always encouraged sticking to ethics from the perspective of the collective.

Actually in the Chinese culture, there is no typical relation or conflict between individualism and collectivism, rather, the relation is between the gentle man and the mean man. The clash between the gentle man and the mean man may not exist in reality, but in morality. Morality marks the difference between the gentle man and the mean man. Hence in the Chinese tradition, the relation between individualism and collectivism turns into a relation between the gentle man and the mean man. Traditionally the protocol of interaction between the gentle man and the mean man is that, the gentle man understands the position of the mean man, acts as the role modal for the mean man, and expects the mean man to progress into a gentle man. This is a status known as the Great Harmony, an ideal society dreamt of by ancient philosophers. According to them, the state shall not take gain as gain, but righteousness as gain. The need of the society is to nurture gentle men and the personality of gentle men leading to a benevolent society.

Confucianism, with Confucius and Mencius' theories as its core, provides a unique living philosophy for the Chinese. The individual is but a tiny drop in the ocean and very insignificant. When there are more people, there is more strength, and unity and solidarity generate power. Confucianism encourages a mindset of "every man has a share of responsibility for the fate of his country". Throughout history, the pursuit of righteous men can be expressed by some sayings or poem lines, including, "To be the first to be concerned with state affairs and the last to enjoy oneself." or "What man was ever immune from death? Let me but leave a loyal heart shining in the pages of history." or "When poor, keep himself virtuous, when rich and prominent, do good deeds for society." These famous lines have been passed on for generations and fully embody the value of the Chinese.

9. 过犹不及，讲究分寸

孔子说："过犹不及"。在孔子看来，事情做得过头了和没有做到位是一样的效果。一般而言，大小诸事，有成有败，有得有失。世间之事，成败得失总有根由。有万千事，即有万千根由。人处世的方法，与做事的成败关系颇大。而"分寸"二字，又在做人做事之法中，近乎锁钥关键。

人和人交往要保持一定的"分寸"，要亲密"有度"。在《论语》中，孔子的学生子游说："当你和领导相处过密时，就要自取其辱了；当你和朋友相处过密时，你们就将要疏远了"。学生又问孔子："那你觉得怎样和人相处呢？"孔子答："相处适度，亲密有间"。在这里我们就可以看到孔子很早就强调人和人相处要保持距离，有分寸，忌讳亲密无间。

"分寸"本来是长度单位，十分一寸，十寸一尺。可在这里已经引申开来，是指说话或做事的适当限度：多少、长短、大小、深浅等等。世间之事物，并非皆多多益善。若说某人心眼儿太多，自然有贬义；而说某人缺心眼儿，当然也不是表扬了。其实，这里的"分寸"，就是唯物辩证法所说的"度"。"度"是一个数量的界限或"临界点"，无论从哪个方向突破了这个"临界点"，事物的性质或形态都会发生变化。因此，掌握好"度"，就成为做人、做事成败的关键。做人、做事任性而为，不管不顾，这样的人有，然而鲜矣！多数人为人、做事，主观上也想恰如其分，只是苦于"分寸"难于把握。

能够掌握分寸，是一件非常不容易的事。分寸隐藏于何处，不是触摸出来的，而是体会出来的。分寸不单纯囿于"情"字，也不单纯拘于"理"字，所谓通情达理者可识分寸，可见"分寸"二字就在情理之间。所以，要学会把握分寸，必须通人情、晓世故，有修养。把握分寸是人的一种综合素质，是内在涵养与外在经验的集中表现。

仔细想来，认识和处理问题讲究分寸、讲究恰到好处的这种对"度"的把握，确实不可轻视。以《三国演义》中的人物为例，关羽是因高傲过度才丢了荆州，惨败麦城；张飞是因对部下惩罚过度而掉了脑袋；司马懿是因谨慎过度才中了诸葛亮的空城计。

把握"度"，一个重要特征就是不走极端。任何事物都有自己相对稳定的存在条件。物极必反。月盈则亏，水满则溢。自然界如此，人类社会亦然。因此，善于把握度的人，无论对己对人，都应注意从总体上把握，做到既不过分，也无不及；不在顺利时忘乎所以，也不在逆境时万念俱灰。表扬人注意不将人捧到天上，批评人也不要将人贬在脚底。同他人发生磕磕碰碰，即使自己正确，理由占到十二分，也需得饶人处且饶人。有些事情涉及多方面的利益冲突，则不要追求绝对的非此即彼，要善于寻找各方利益的衔接处与平衡点。

要想准确把握"度"，就要具备良好的道德修养。无论在社会还是在家庭中，要既不"缺位"、又不"越位"；既要努力把事情做足做够，又不要过分；既要经得起表扬，又能坦然接受批评；既能面对鲜花、掌声，又能装得下误解、委屈。

在日常生活中，如果你能把握分寸，说话有度，交往有节，办事伸缩得当，人们就会通情达理地承领你的要求，尊重你的体面，满足你的愿望。如果你不懂分寸，说话冒失，举止失体，不识深浅，不知厚薄，那么你的人缘肯定不好，处世也会处处留下败笔。所以，掌握分寸是为人处世的普遍规则，是获得好人缘的第一准则。

A Sense of Propriety

Confucius said that to go beyond the mark is as bad as to fall short of it. Thus, Confucius thought that doing something that goes beyond the limit counts no more than not doing enough. Generally speaking, whether it is a big thing or small thing, the results can only be to succeed or fail — to gain or lose. There are many reasons behind success and failure, thousands and thousands of reasons. Yet, whether one succeeds or fails is influenced considerably by the skills one uses in dealing with the problem. "Propriety" is the key to successful interactions between oneself and other people.

Interacting with somebody should involve a tactfulness that avoids things that would offend them. This is illustrated in the book *The Analects of Confucius*, in which a student of Confucius said: "When you are too close to your leader, it is the same as inviting humiliation; when you are too close to a friend, the two of you will soon drift apart." The students then asked: "What is your way of dealing with others?" Confucius answered: "Get on appropriately with others, stay close but keep a distance." Here we should note that

Confucius had emphasized long ago that people who live together should keep some distance, and avoid "being on very intimate terms with each other."

The Chinese word for propriety is to have "fencun." "Fen" and "cun" are units of length, ten "fen" are equal to one "cun," and ten "cun" are equal to one "chi." But, its literal meaning is extended in this context, here it refers to a proper limitation when people deal with other people and things: more or less, long or short, big or small, and deep or shallow, etc. It is not the case that everything or every situation in the world follows the rule: the more the better. If we say that someone is too sensitive, it is, of course, derogatory. And, if we say that someone seems insensitive, that does not count as praise. So, what tact or "propriety" means here is the "range" in materialistic dialectics. "Range" constitutes a boundary or "critical point" in the quality or quantity. It does not matter from which direction this boundary is broken, then the nature or pattern of the thing will be completely changed. Thus, learning how to handle the "limit" is the key to one's success or failure. Today there are only a few people who are completely unrestrained, and disregard the consequences of their conduct or behavior. Most people want to act appropriately when dealing with people and things, but they suffer from a lack of knowledge of the proper limits for speech or action.

It is not easy to develop the skills necessary to be tactful, one has to learn by experience. Propriety is situated between what is rational and what is feeling, yet it is not purely based on "feeling" or "reason." So, if one wants to learn to grasp propriety, one has to understand human relationships, know the ways of the world, and have considerable sophistication. The skill of propriety arises from a wide-rang of qualities, it is the concentrated expression of a person's internal virtue of patience and the external influences that result from a rich body of experience.

If we think carefully, we shall know that we should take the tactful way of recognizing and settling problems, be particular and balance things just right. Examples from several characters in a historical novel, *Romance of the Three Kingdoms*, demonstrate this point. Guan Yu lost Jingzhou City because he was over arrogant, and he also tragically lost Maicheng City. Zhang Fei lost his head because he punished his officers excessively for a minor reason. Sima Yi failed to recognize Zhuge Liang's stratagem of the Empty City because of his extremely suspicious nature.

To handle "tact," it is important not to go to extremes.

All things have their own comparatively balance and will tilt toward the one direction or the other under the influence of extremes. The natural principle is like a crescent moon that follows the full moon or like a bowl that is too full and overflows. The natural environment works in this way, human society should be the same. So, a person skilled at being tactful, either with himself or others, should pay attention to the overall circumstances, not trying to do too much nor failing to do enough. One must not be carried away by one's successes nor have one's hopes dashed by adversity. When you praise someone, you should not raise them to the sky. When you criticize someone, you cannot walk all over them. Although you may be absolutely correct about a thing, when you and others disagree, you should still forgive for the other's errors. If the matter involves a conflict of interest, you shouldn't seek an absolute black or white solution, but find the common ground by which to share equal profit.

To be tactful effectively one must have a good moral bearing, no matter whether one is at home or in a social situation, one should neither lose one's position nor overstep one's bounds. One should try hard to fulfill the mission without going too far. One who can stand to receive commendations and rewards can also stand criticisms as well. One should be able to accept flowers as well as bear misunderstandings and injustice.

In your daily life, if you can approach a situation tactfully, with appropriate words, and interact with people morally, dealing with all things in a suitable way, people will accept your requests, respect your dignity and help solve the problem in a reasonable way. On the other hand, if you don't understand tact, speak rudely, interact with people without manners, and behave inappropriately, you will lose people's friendship and fail in whatever mission you attempt. Hence, being tactful is a universal law of dealing with the world and is the first measure of a "good person."

10. 中国人的时间观念

中国人与大多数东方人一样，时间观念与西方人是有所不同的。过去的中国人如果与人相约的话，常用的口语就是：上午吧、下午吧、晚上吧，较少用具体几时来回答。

这种时间观念的形成与中国人自古以来的生活方式是分不开的。中国在历史上一直以农业为经济主体，长期的农业自然经济形成了平民百姓日出而作、日落而息的生活习惯，他们是白天靠太阳，夜晚靠更夫，因此对时间无法精确计算。过去中国人常用"时辰"作为计时单位。一天一夜共十二个时辰，一个时辰合现在的两个小时。长期下来，人们便逐渐养成了悠闲宽松的时间观念。

除了生活方式，这种时间观念的形成也有着很深的文化渊源。中国文化自古注重人与自然的和谐，"天人合一"是中国哲学的基本精神之一。中国文化赋予了时间更多抽象、神秘的含义，凡事要成功必须讲究"天时"、"地利"和"人和"。"天时"往往通过某种人们不可知的力量影响事物的发展。此种思维方式使中国文化传统非常注重"时"的顺背，因而形成了国人对时间的感知带有浓厚的主观色彩，受客观时间的约束较少。换言之，无论自然天体、物质运动形成的时间结构如何，它终归是为了人的目的和价值运行的。人是把握时间的主体，时间要为人服务。时间的快慢、松紧、进退皆以人的目的和感觉为基础。

这种时间观念体现在生活中的各个方面。例如，太极拳是中国具有代表性意义的武术项目，架式平稳，动作舒缓，讲求一个"慢"字，以慢攻急，以柔克刚，充分体现出中国人的民族性格。再如中国传统的中医，治疗方式也不像西医那样直指患处以图速效，而是着眼于人体的整个生理机能的平衡，以循序渐进的温补调养为治疗宗旨。

与这种时间意识相伴而生的，一是中国人对待时间的随意性和宽容态度。如中国人欢迎别人随时来访，以体现出一家人的亲切与随意。对被迫放下手头的事接待来访者也习以为常。传统社会中，大多数中国人在登门拜访时，谈话时间的长短也全凭当时的气氛与兴致。这种时间观念使得勤俭节约的中国人在时间上比较慷慨。在礼仪用语中常可以听到这样的话："请慢走"、"请慢用"、"各位慢吃"等。

二是中国人对时间采用一种"适时观"。在必要时自能随其所需而伸缩。庄子创立了"安时"说,即安于或顺应于时间的自然而然的流程。儒家提倡"适时"说,即不论做什么事都要讲究"时机"和"时运"。在各种矛盾运动的时间流程中,我们应当根据矛盾运动及其时间进程的不同情况,适时地抓住时机去"执"其中,"用"其中。因而中国人在时间的使用上显得灵活、有弹性,不那么呆板。此外,在时间的延伸方面没有那么刻板。反映在商务活动中,如果双方在约定的时间中没有生意上的进展,人们也会继续交流,增进相互的了解。此外,中国人一般会约定开始的时间,很少会明确规定结束的时间。通常,人们会在双方认为合适的时间结束约会。从这点上来说,中国人是时间的主人。

而西方文化采取的则是"二元"的思维模式,将主体与客体,人与对象、自然明确分开,研究主体与客体的相互关系。这与中国人强调天人合一,主客一体的思维方式不同。这种哲学观念使西方人对时间的认识更加注重对自然时间和物理时间的探讨,具有很大的客观性。在西方文化中,年、月、日是严格按照天体星球的运动来计算的。西方人大约在17世纪就掌握了比较精确的计时工具,所以西方人计时往往精确至分和秒。有人曾开玩笑地讲,一名德国人发请帖,上面写开宴会的时间是12:03分。这在我们看来是十分可笑的,但这却说明了他们的时间观念，开宴会的时间一分也不能差。

尽管中国人传统的时间观念具有缓慢、随意等特征，但面对中国社会经济的高速发展和生活节奏加快的冲击，中国人现在的时间观念正在发生变化，主观性减弱、客观性增强。这种变化顺应了经济全球化的趋势，对社会经济的发展有促进作用。但从人性本身来说，人就应该是时间的主宰。应该说中国传统的时间观念更具人文色彩。也许未来人类回归自然的时候，中国传统的时间观念会重新得到大家的青睐呢！

The Concept of Time in the Chinese Culture

Similar to most Eastern people, the Chinese have a different concept of time compared with Westerners. In the past, when making an appointment, the Chinese would usually say, "let's meet in the morning", or "in the afternoon", or "in the evening". They would seldom specify at which specific hour they'd like to meet.

Such a concept of time has been formed along with Chinese lifestyles since ancient time. In history, China's economy mainly relied on agriculture, and the living habits of the Chinese were formed in the agricultural economy such as getting up with the rising of the sun, and going to bed with the setting of the sun. Ancient Chinese people told the time of the day by the movement of the sun, and during the night by the regular beating of the watches by the night watchmen. Time for them was not accurate. Traditionally for the Chinese there were 12 periods in a day, with one period as roughly two hours, and the Chinese were very relaxed in terms of time.

In addition to its origins in the cultural lifestyle, the concept of time has profound roots in natural and environmental events. The Chinese culture pays great attention to the harmony of man and nature, and the unity of man and nature is one of the basic ideas of Chinese philosophy. The concept of time has been endowed with abstract and mythical connotations, and the success of anything was believed to be dependent on "timing and opportunity, geographical advantage, as well as unity and coordination among people". "Timing and opportunity" influences the evolvement of things through certain forces unknown to human beings. Such a mindset has resulted in the traditional attention to good or bad "timing and opportunity". As a result, the concept of time for the Chinese has a strong subjective and wishful flavor, which is seldom restrained by the objective concept of time. In other words, no

matter how the planets follow their courses and how the material movements are, for Chinese people time serves for the purpose and value of human beings. The master of time is man and time is at the service of man. The tempo of time is based on the purposes or feelings of human beings.

Such a concept of time is embodied in many aspects of life. Taiji Boxing, for example, is representative of Chinese martial arts and has very stable and slow movement of postures. Taiji believes that slowness curbs rapidness, and mildness subdues strength, which to a large extent shows the character of the Chinese nation. Take the traditional Chinese medicine as another example, unlike Western medicine, Chinese medicine does not pursue an immediate cure of illness and thus a quick recovery of the patient, but an overall balance of the physical functions of the human body, and the treatments are centered on the gradual and progressive adjustment and nourishment.

A casualness and tolerance towards time accompanies the concept of time. Chinese people welcome friends to visit them "at any time they like", to show their closeness and casualness. They are not offended by visitors without appointment even if the visit disturbs them. In the past, a visit might take as long as the hosts and the guests liked. Such a concept of time made the Chinese very generous with their time, as a contrast they are thrifty with many other things. Among polite expressions, there are literally "Please walk slowly", "Please eat slowly", all meaning to take time and enjoy oneself.

The Chinese people are also flexible toward time according to their needs. Zhuang Zi, an ancient philosopher believed in "adaptive to time", that is, to be adaptive or follow the natural trend of time, and Confucius believed in "good timing" and "opportunity". Good opportunity is to be seized in the process of the movement of contradictions and their different timing to reach one's goal. As a result, the Chinese are not rigid toward time. In business activities, if certain agreement is not reached within a time limit, both parties usually will not give up but continue to negotiate and communicate for better understanding. And for gatherings, the Chinese decide the starting time, but they seldom specify the ending time. A gathering ends when both parties feel proper. In this sense, people are the masters of time.

But Western philosophy is one of dualism, which studies the relationship of the subject and the object, and divides clearly between the subject and the object, between man and nature. This is a different approach from the Chinese philosophy of harmony of the subject and the object, of man and

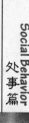

nature. Westerners stress the objectivity of time from a perspective of the natural time and physical time. In the Western culture, year, month and day are accurately calculated according to the movement of celestial bodies and planets. In the West, precision tools to keep time were mastered in about the 17th century, and time had long been calculated to minutes and seconds. One joke regarding the time concept of the German people, who are known to be very accurate and strict on time, describes a request that a banquet begin at 12:03. This sounds ridiculous to Chinese people. However, it manifests the time concept of the Westerners as shown in the accuracy of time when the banquet starts.

Albeit the traditional concept of time for the Chinese regards time in a slow and casual manner, the current concept of time is changing with the fast social-economic development and quickening tempo of living. It attaches more importance to objectivity than subjectivity, following the trend of economic globalization and playing a positive role in social-economic development. Yet from the perspective of human nature, human beings should be in charge of time. We should admit that the traditional concept of time in China is endowed with more senses of humanity and may regain people's favor as we return to nature in the future.

11. 人情与法律

　　不管是在法制健全还是不健全的国家，任何执法人员都必须做到"法不容情"，这点是必须的，否则社会就无法正常运转，人民就会不服政府的管理。但是在中国人看来，法律虽然是不可以违背的，但是有些时候是不是可以讲讲人情，从轻处理，以实现"情与法的变通"或者"法与情的兼容"呢？

　　让我们看看历史。在古代春秋时期，中原有个小诸侯国，名叫叶国，国君叶公仰慕孔子的名声，有一次见到孔子，高兴地对孔子说："我想请教您一个问题，如何才能治理好国家呢？"孔子说："能够做到国内的百姓满意，别国的百姓前来归附，这就是治理的成功。"叶公还向孔子讲述了自己国家的社会现象，说："我们那里有位正直的人，他的父亲偷了别人的羊，他便前去告发，可谓为人正直。"孔子听了不以为然，说："我们这里和你们那儿不同，我们这里正直人的标准和你们有差异，我们这儿的正直人的做法是，父亲替儿子隐瞒罪过，儿子为父亲隐瞒罪过，这样做，我们才认为是正直。"孔子的原话是:"父为子隐,子为父隐,直在其中矣!"这种"正直"的观念对中国后世的法制产生了深远的影响,也就是后世所谓的"法律不外乎人情"的渊源。若在法治社会中,人人遵守法律,父亲盗窃,儿子告发,并没有错,是合法又合理的事情。但是从人情上衡量,就存在问题了。父子关系应当说是恩情最深的社会关系。如果儿子告发犯罪的父亲,用亲情的尺度为标准来裁判,那么,这个儿子就是不孝之子,就要遭受社会伦理道德的谴责。这时候众人都会站在亲情的阵营中指责那个"逆子"。

人情因素对法治建设的影响在中国表现得非常特殊,这与中国的历史传统是密不可分的。古代社会中的主流文化是儒家学说,而这个为统治者所极力推崇的思想,核心在于维护古代的礼教制度。孔子曾说:"周监于二代,郁郁乎文哉,吾从周。"意思是:"周朝的礼仪制度借鉴于夏、商二代,是多么丰富多彩啊。我遵从周朝的制度。"他的得意门生颜渊问怎样做才是"仁",孔子告诉他:"克制自己,一切都照着礼的要求去做,这就是仁。一旦这样做了,天下的一切就都归于仁了。实行仁德,完全在于自己,难道还在于别人吗?"颜渊说:"请问应该如何做。"孔子说:"不合于礼的不要看,不合于礼的不要听,不合于礼的不要说,不合于礼的不要做。"因此,古代中国社会就用三纲五常之类的礼仪规范来约束人们的言行,而不是把法律作为处理案件的依据。

中国产生这样的现象是由古代社会的生产方式所决定的。长期以来，中国古代社会的统治者执行的是重农抑商的经济政策，农业是社会的命脉，而商业则被视为不能产生社会效益的末业，被大家所歧视。汉高祖"令贾人不得衣丝乘车"，惠帝、高后"为天下初定，复驰商贾之律，然市井子孙亦不得仕宦为吏。"于是，自给自足的小农经济成了社会的基本存在状况。小农经济是封闭的经济，人们生活在一个很狭小的范围和圈子内，每一个人都处在特定的熟人社会里，形成了亲属血缘关系的宗族制度。个人、家庭、宗族，是构成国家的基本因素。我们知道，人情是亲属血缘关系的必然产物，因此，维系这样的社会生活，需要的是礼仪，而不是法律，人情渗透到社会政治、生活的各个层面，是再正常不过的事情了。所以有的研究者认为：中国古代的法律就好比漂浮在情理的海洋上的冰山，法官作出的任何一个判决，归根到底，都有意无意地受着情理的影响。

人情是人与人相处的一种贴心的关系和感觉，而法律是一种约束和限制这种关系的手段和尺度。人们制订法律是来约束大家的，大家要认识法律，遵守法律，违反了法律就有可能犯罪。可是在许多时候，人们不得不面对情与法的冲突。

曾听一位从美国留学归国的朋友说了这么一件事。留学时，一个中国餐馆的老板娘去商店给四岁女儿买鞋。女儿在丈夫驾驶的车里等候妈妈，他们急着要送女儿上托儿所。老板娘在鞋店左挑右挑，一看时间不多了，便拿起一双鞋匆匆走出店门，结果警报响了，她这才想起竟然没有付款。她急忙向店员解释，并请边上的中国留学生翻译。但商店却坚持要起诉她。这位"海归"帮她去法庭做翻译。法官很忙，他们花了四五个小时，等来的是不到五分钟的出庭受审。最后判决是：考虑到这位母亲是第一次犯这样的错误，私拿的只是一双便宜的童鞋，如果半年内不再犯同样的罪，这次留下的案底就自动消除。从这个小事的结果，我们不难看出西方人确实是"法不容情"的。如果同样的事情在中国发生，那母亲当场稍作解释，诚诚恳恳付了钱就没事了。鞋店老板也不会为这样的"小事"报警上法庭，最多支付点处罚金了事。

　　中国是一个情理大国，但讲情理并不会被认为是破坏了法律的尊严。在法律规定的基础上，情理成为了一种司法态度、一种司法技术。"以情理来考虑法律问题，而不是抛弃法律讲究情理"，这也是发展中的中国一个特色吧。

Feelings and the Law

In a country observing rule of law, whether the legal system is sound or not, it is essential that law enforcement be impartial to personal feelings. Otherwise the people will not accept the administration of the government and society will not be run consistently. Regardless, the Chinese people pay great attention to the appropriate adaptations and accommodations between feelings and the law even though the law can never be broken. Yes, the law shall be abided by, but should not the punishment be executed in the slightest possible way, with careful consideration of feelings?

Chinese history provides examples of this philosophy. In the Spring and Autumn Period there was a small state in the middle of China called the State of Ye. The Duke of Ye highly regarded Confucius and asked him when they met, "I have a question for you. How shall I run my state in a good way?" Confucius answered, "A successful run of the state is to satisfy your people and attract people from other states to submit to your rule." The Duke of Ye told Confucius of something that happened in his state. "We have a man who

Social Behavior
处事篇

lodged an accusation against his father when his father stole other people's sheep. We think the man showed integrity." Confucius however disagreed, "I have a different idea of integrity from you. Integrity is that the father conceals his son's offense, and the son conceals his father's offense." Confucius' concept of integrity laid a profound influence on the rule of law in the Chinese society, and served as the origin of the mindset of "The law is within the consideration of feelings." There is nothing wrong in a society of rule of law that if father steals, his son accuses him. But measured by human feelings, it is problematic. The relation between father and son is the deepest running relationship in a society. If the son accuses his father who committed an offense, he is a son without filial piety. He will be condemned or criticized under the standard of social ethics and human feelings.

The factor of feelings is particularly influential in the creation of laws in China, as closely linked to Chinese tradition. The mainstay of culture in ancient China was Confucianism which had been promoted by generations of rulers. The core of it was to safeguard the ethical code of the ancient society. Confucius once said, "The ethical code of the Zhou Dynasty uses that of Xia and Shang dynasties for reference and is very rich and colorful. I myself follow Zhou's code and system." Yan Yuan, one of his best disciples asked him how one could become benevolent. Confucius' answer was, "Try to restrain yourself, and follow an ethical code whatever you do, then you become a benevolent man. And everything in the world will submit to benevolence. To be benevolent is a personal thing and totally up to oneself, not up to other people. " Yan Yuan asked about rules to follow when trying to be benevolent, Confucius answered, "Do not look at what is against the ethical code, do not listen to what is against the ethical code, do not say what is against the ethical code and do not do what is against the ethical code." The ancient Chinese society followed the three cardinal guides (ruler guides subject, father guides son and husband guides wife), and the five constant virtues (benevolence, righteousness, propriety, wisdom and fidelity), not laws and regulations.

Such phenomenon in China has been formed by the way of production in ancient China. For a very long period of time in history, a policy of preference for agriculture and distaste for commerce dominated. Agriculture was regarded as the lifeline of the traditional society. Commerce, as the last trade that could not bring about any social benefit, was thus discriminated against. Emperor Gao of the Han Dynasty (206 BC–220 AD) ordered that "Merchants may not dress in silk and ride carriages." Emperor Hui and Queen Gao ordered that "The country is now in peace and commercial activities can be restored, but merchants shall not become officials." As a result, the self-sustained small scale agriculture economy became the standard of the society. Living in the enclosed economic environment and thus a narrow social network, each individual lived within a fixed proximity to people he knew and interpersonal relationship was one of kinship. The basic elements of the society were person, family and clan. Feelings became the natural result of kinship and blood relationship. In such a society what was needed was an ethical code, not laws to be universally followed. It was normal for feelings to penetrate to all aspects of social-political life. Some scholars think that law in ancient China was like icebergs floating in the sea of feelings. Any decisions and judgments by officials were influenced by feelings, intentionally or unintentionally.

Feelings were a bond for people in their communication, and law is a measurement for guiding and restraining interpersonal communications. Going against the law is committing offense. But more often than not, people have to face the confrontation between feeling and law.

A Chinese friend of mine who studied in the United

States told me a true story that happened in the States. A woman who ran a Chinese restaurant with her husband went to a shop to buy her 4-year-old daughter a pair of shoes on the way to the daughter's kindergarten, with her husband and daughter sitting in the car waiting for her. The wife spent some time choosing the shoes and then in such a hurry she took the shoes and made her way out of the shop. The moment she stepped out of the entrance, the alarm rung. She realized that she forgot to pay. The shop attendant refused to listen to her explanation and sued her. My friend was her interpreter at court. They spent four or five hours at court for all the formalities, and the verdict of the court took only five minutes. The verdict was, because it was the first time for her to commit such an offense, and what she took was a pair of cheap shoes, her behavior was recorded and would be automatically diminished only when she would not commit a similar offense within six months. From this example we can see that in the Western society, there is no room for feelings in terms of law. If something similar happens in China, the woman needs only to explain herself and pay for the goods. The shop may ask for a fine, but will not sue her in court.

China is a country whose people believe that feelings have a role to play. However, the consideration of feelings

shall not be regarded as a way to reduce the esteem of the law, but rather as an attitude or technique to supplement law and regulations. It can be deemed as a Chinese characteristic to grapple with legal issues from the perspective of feelings, but not to take account of feelings for the purpose of getting rid of the law.

家庭篇

Family

12. 以家为重的中国人

中国传统社会是一个农业社会，家庭是最重要的生产和消费的运作单位。家庭，确切地说，是家族，成为中国文化中一个最重要的柱石，中国的文化大都是以家族观念为基础建立起来的。中国的传统文化观念中正是先有了家族观念才有了人道观念。

家庭本位的思想无疑是中国人最重视的思想之一，这与西方所倡导的个体本位截然不同。一个传统社会中的中国人，他的身份、地位、价值、权利、义务和责任，都是和他的家庭、家族紧密联系在一起的，两者不可分割，一损俱损，一荣俱荣。为了维护家庭的和谐与稳定，千百年来，中国古代思想家都在提倡"家和睦邻、仁爱礼让、勤俭持家"等道德原则，"父慈子孝、夫义妇顺、兄友弟恭"等道德规范在中国人的心中早已根深蒂固。

从中国人的日常用语中不难看出，中国人不管是习惯使然还是约定俗成，许多用语中都含有"家"的元素。公是公家，国是国家，全体是大家，别人是人家，自己是自家，同姓是本家。还有各种职业的称呼：农家、渔家、船家、东家、店家、商家、行家、专家。这足以显示出，家在中国人的心目中的地位是多么重要。

传统的中国家庭孕育于华夏民族独特的生存土壤和文化环境，因而家庭伦理呈现出区别于其他民族的鲜明特征。首先，传统中国人以家族生活为活动范围，家族至上的群体意识成为传统家庭伦理的核心精神。家庭和谐是以个人利益无条件服从家族群体利益来实现的。其次，在等级服从的家长制家庭中，家内人际关系以与父亲的亲疏远近而依次排序，形成等级差序的人际格局，家庭成员尊卑地位分明。

总之，家庭是中国人生活的重中之重，时刻在发挥着作用。中国人看重亲情，常说"血浓于水"。以血缘为基础的亲情关系是中国人生活中不可或缺的部分。"家庭是心灵最后的港湾"，这无疑也是在强调家庭是个人最终的归宿。虽然社会经历着巨大变革，中国人的家庭结构也发生了很大变化，但许多人仍然尊重以家庭和谐为中心的传统观念，他们愿意投入更多精力维持家庭，而相应地，他们也需要来自家庭更多的支持和帮助。要想了解中国人，就一定要清楚家庭在他们心目中的重要位置。

Holding Dear the Family

The traditional Chinese society was an agricultural society, and family was the most important social unit with regards to production and consumption. Family is a mainstay of Chinese culture with the traditional Chinese humanism culture originating from the family concept, and a majority of the Chinese culture is built on the concept of family.

The biggest difference between the Chinese and Western culture is that the Chinese consider family to be most important while Westerners consider individualism to be the priority. In the Chinese society, the social importance of any individual is indivisible from his family, be it his blood relations or a similar social unit he relies on. The social identity, value, responsibility, rights and obligations of the individuals are all closely related to his family clans and relations in the traditional Chinese society. The Chinese people have gotten used to this traditional concept that has existed for thousands of years and have been very careful with their words and behaviors to follow the social norms.

The importance of family is manifested in the formation

家庭篇 Family

of some common Chinese words and expressions. Many nouns include the family element (which is *jia* in Chinese), including "public" (*gong jia*), "state" (*guo jia*), "all" (*da jia*), "others" (*ren jia*), "self" (*zi jia*), "people of the same family name" (*ben jia*), "farmer" (*nong jia*), "fisherman" (*yu jia*), "boatman" (*chuan jia*), "host" (*dong jia*), "shopkeeper" (*dian jia*), "merchant" (*shang jia*) and "expert" (*hang jia, zhuan jia*). These all reflect the importance of family in Chinese people's minds.

The traditions observed by Chinese families were born from China's unique cultural background, and China's family ethics are different from other countries. First, family was traditionally the major activity sphere of the people, and the ideology of family clan priority was the core of Chinese family ethic. Family harmony required that individual interests bow to family interests unconditionally. Second, in the Chinese patriarchal system, the standing between relatives, as well as their precedence in the family were all decided by their relation with the father, the male dominator of the family.

In a word, family is of crucial importance in the life of Chinese people and constantly plays a strong role. Chinese people value the emotional tie and often say that "blood is thicker than water". The affectionate feeling based upon ties of blood is an indispensible part of the life of Chinese people. "Family is the last bay of the soul" undoubtedly emphasizes that family is one's most reliable settling place. Although the Chinese society is undergoing massive transformations and considerable changes have taken place in the structure of Chinese families, many people still honor the traditional view which prioritizes harmony in the family. As such, they are willing to devote more energy to maintaining the household and accordingly, they need the family to provide more support and assistance in return. Being well aware of the importance of family is an important step in understanding the minds of Chinese people.

家
庭
篇
Family

13. 男主外 & 女主内

儒家思想是几千年中国文化的主脉，也是中国古代社会的精神缩影。孔子极力主张建立一个尊卑有序的社会。在家庭内，他主张男子治外而女子治内的分工合作，也就是我们常说的"男主外，女主内"。在这样性别分工的传统观念中，男性需要承担起养护全家成员的责任，尤其在经济方面。与此相对应的，他们在家庭中的权威也是绝对的。在儒家关于男女分工的经典话语中，男性通常是作为"天"而存在的，要求女性要做到"夫唱妇随"。而女性的职责则主要局限于家庭内部：伺候公婆、抚育孩子、操持家务等等。虽然乡村妇女经常也会在生产活动中扮演一定的角色，但这并不影响男女分工的主体格局。正是由于男女所扮演的角色不同，所承担的生活负担不同，并且受传统的"夫为妻纲"的伦理纲常的价值观的影响，特别是男子继承权在宗族传承中的神圣地位和不可替代性，决定了家庭中的男性权力往往会优于女权。

在中国以血缘关系为纽带的宗法社会的基础上，社会成为家国一体的社会组织结构。在这样的宗法社会里，家始终是社会和国家的坚实基础，个人消融于家之中。君权与父权合一，"家庭没有两个主人，国家没有两个君主"。在家庭中以父亲为核心，父权高于一切，实行家长制；国家则是以君主为核心，皇权高于一切，实行君主专制。"男主外"的分工地位有其坚实的社会基础和制度渊源。

而在此基础上，中国传统社会对女性也有其独特的概括。繁体字"婦"字本身代表的意思就是一个手拿扫帚打扫和保持房子清洁的人。也就是说，古代中国把妇女称做厨房的主人，而后随之演变为主持家务的人。

中国的封建思想一贯主张"三从四德"。所谓"三从"，就是说一个中国妇女在她出嫁之前要听从父亲的吩咐；当她结婚后要听从丈夫的吩咐；当她成为寡妇时，她又必须为自己的子女活着。只有如此恪尽职守的女性才是一个完美女性。所谓的"四德"，就是说女子首先应该谦虚含蓄、纯洁坚贞，有无可指责的品行和完美无缺的举止；其次，女子要言辞谨慎，不能使用粗鲁的语言；再次，女子不需有太过美丽的容貌，但是穿着打扮要恰到好处、整洁干净，不能让别人在背后指指点点；最后，女子不需要有专门的技能，但是她们应该勤快而专心致力于纺织和家务，尤其是家中有客人时更要表现得体，不能给家庭丢脸。

这种宗法式的伦理道德长久而深远地左右着中国人的社会心理和行为规范。当每一个家庭中的男女双方都完成自己的责任和义务，那么双方就会获得自己应有的地位和权利，共同维持家庭的稳定和和睦。即使社会发展到主张男女平等的今天，我们也不难看到，中国仍有很多家庭是由男性来负担家庭的经济责任的。

　　不过，随着经济的发展和时代的进步，越来越多的中国家庭，特别是年轻一代，夫妻双方共同负担家庭生活的情况也在逐年增加。中国这种传统、落后的家庭观念正逐渐被人们所抛弃。根据最新一项调查报告，随着越来越多的女性走出家庭参加社会实践，她们在家庭中的权利也越来越大，夫妻共同决定甚至主要由妻子决定的比例达到 60% — 70%。越来越多的女性可以自主决定个人事务。特别值得注意的是，在中国农村，由于有不少男性进入城市寻找工作，农村妇女承担了家庭的全部劳动和生活。责任增大的同时，妇女在家庭中的权力也大大加强，她们的自信心和应对各种复杂事务的能力也明显提高。超过 2/3 以上的中国女性对目前的婚姻家庭、物质、精神生活表示满意。

Men and Women Play Different Roles

The Confucian philosophy, as the main pulse of Chinese culture, suggests a social order with men superior to women. The husband is responsible to handle external affairs, and the wife to take charge of home affairs. This traditional social division puts the family support, especially economic support, and outside home responsibilities on the men. To balance their contribution to the family, they have absolute authority at home, and are considered to have the power of heaven in the family. The wife is supposed to be her husband's echo, and her main responsibilities are to take care of the elders, to educate the children, and to handle the house chores. In rural areas, women also do some farm work, but their main responsibilities are focused at home. Because of the different family and social roles of men and women, and the unchanging inheritance power of the males, men have always been superior to women in the traditional Chinese family.

The Chinese society is built on the basis of such a patriarchal system emphasizing blood relations. Family unity is the foundation of social and national stability, and individual

家庭篇 Family

interests have been ignored. The power of father in the family and the monarchial power were integrated in Chinese history, and as the Chinese saying goes, "There are never two monarchs in one state, and never two home masters in one family." The father is the core of the family and his power is the highest. In the feudal system, the emperor is the core of the government and his power is superior to anyone and anything else. The dominating power of the male has a solid social background and systemic guarantee.

The Confucius philosophy considers a gentle, refined and kind-hearted female the ideal woman. The Chinese character for woman is actually composed of two parts, female on the left and a broom on the right, suggesting a woman keeping the room clean. In ancient China, women were called the "kitchen keeper", and later changed to "one who masters house chores".

The Chinese ethic requires woman to follow three obediences and four virtues. The three obediences are: obedience to father before marriage, to husband after marriage and to son after the death of her husband. Only those who understand and fulfill all these duties are considered the perfect woman. The four virtues refer to morality, proper speech, modest manner and diligent work. She shall be modest, pure and faithful, be careful with every speech and behavior, never using rude words and always knowing when to stop talking, never gossiping. She doesn't have to be very beautiful but must be clean and properly dressed, doesn't have to have a professional skill but must be diligent and good at knitting and house chores. When there are guests visiting the house, she shall know how to behave and not lose face for the family.

The deep-rooted patriarchal virtues have big influence over Chinese people's social psychology and norms of behavior. Men and women try to fulfill their rights and obligations at home, to keep their social and family position, and as a result to sustain family stability and harmony. In present China, when men and women enjoy equal rights and freedom, we can see that in many families, the husbands still bear the main economic responsibility.

However, with the development of the economy and the advancement of the times, the number of families, especially those among the younger generation, in which the couple share the family costs together, is increasing on a yearly basis. The traditional and backward family concept in China is gradually being abandoned. According to a very recent survey, as more women leave their homes and take part in social practice, they are gaining even more rights in the family.

家庭篇 Family

Decisions made together as a couple or mainly by the wife account for 60-70% of the total and there are more and more women who choose to decide personal affairs for themselves. It is noteworthy that in rural areas of China, as many men move to the cities to seek jobs, the women thus assume all the responsibility of daily family life. As their responsibility grows, so does their rights in the family. Furthermore, their self-confidence and the ability to deal with various kinds of complex affairs have improved significantly. Over two-thirds of the Chinese women are satisfied with their current marriage, family, material and spiritual life.

14. 中国式婚姻

　　婚姻对于每个人来说都是生活的重要组成部分之一。尤其在以家族本位为传统的中国社会，结婚和丧葬是一个家庭的两件重大事情，其中结婚更是关系到家庭血统的传承，其重要性自然不可小视。

　　在家族利益至上的中国传统社会里，家庭的存在对于个人具有决定性作用。因此，在传统的宗法社会里，一个人结不结婚，什么时候结婚，和什么人结婚，都不是由自己决定的，也不由自己选择。结婚并不仅仅是男女双方当事人的事，而是他们双方家族的事，关系着双方家族的血统传承、荣辱兴衰。因此，男女双方常常被迫按照"父母之命，媒妁之言"去例行公事，而他们的情感则常常以会损害家族的利益为由而被抑制或排斥。

　　那么这种不以个人意愿为基础的中国式婚姻曾经如此受到人们重视的原因又何在呢？通过上文相关内容的介绍，我们可以看出，中国传统婚姻的目的有四个：一是尽义务。所谓"男大当婚，女大当嫁"，这是中国人历来的观念。不仅如此，社会还对结婚的上限年龄有一定的规定，认为男子在三十岁以前、女子在二十岁以前应该成婚，否则对个人和家庭来说都不是一件光彩的事情。二是双方家族结成血缘关系，扩大家族的关系网络。三是为男方家族继承血统，"生儿育女，传宗接代"，这无疑是最重要的目的之一。四是过日子，尤其是在看重家庭对个人影响的中国，男女双方只要门当户对，有媒有保，就能够结婚。结婚后两人能够互相依靠，互相帮助，团结协助，共建家业，这就是一个好家庭了。

从这几个目的看，我们可以了解，中国人过去的婚姻中，生儿育女、传宗接代才是中国式婚姻的主要目的。在这种夫妻关系中，传统的中国人对待婚姻的态度只是被迫接受被社会大众所认同的常规和现实，而非出自自身的需求以及夫妻双方感情的相互吸引。这种中国式的婚姻完全忽略了人在精神层面的需求，压抑了人性和欲望。

不过随着社会发展和人类文明的进步，科学、民主、自由、平等的观念慢慢深入人心，如今的中国人已经破除了旧式婚姻的束缚，自由恋爱、男女平等的思想已深得大众认可。

同时，现代中国家庭结构也发生了巨大的变迁。过去传统的四世同堂大家庭已转变为夫妻加上子女的小家庭，家族观念的影响在不断减弱。家庭中男女的地位日

趋平等使绝大部分妻子和丈夫一样从事着社会工作，并
具有一定的经济自主能力。夫妻关系日益成为家庭关系
的核心，其中爱情是缔结婚姻关系的根本前提，也是评
价婚姻关系及其生活品质的重要道德标准。

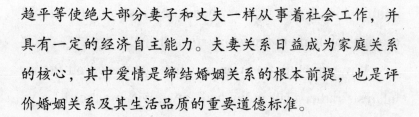

Marriage Development in China

Marriage plays a most important role in one's life, especially in the home-centered Chinese society. Chinese people consider marriages and funerals as two very important events in the family. Marriage is important because it is a matter of carrying on the ancestral line.

As the Chinese traditionally place family interests in a vital position, family relations play a decisive role in one's life. In the traditional patriarchal society, one did not have the freedom to decide when and with whom to get married. Marriage was not a matter of the two individuals, but of the two families, as marriage was related to the carrying of ancestral lines of the two families, as well as the reputation and fate of the two families. As a result, the man and woman were often forced to act as a routine by obeying the will of the parents and proposal of the matchmaker. While the

家庭篇 Family

natural love between them had to be restrained to avoid causing any harm to the family interests.

Why was this tradition of marriages based on family interests rather than individual's own will practiced for so long? From the above introductions we can see that traditional Chinese marriage had four purposes: First, to fulfill one's obligation to the family. "Upon coming of age, every male should take a wife and every female a husband" is a concept long been held by the Chinese. Furthermore, according to Chinese tradition, men must get married before 30 years old and women before 20, and it was usually considered shameful for the family if the children were still single by that age limit. Second, to create a tie of blood and expand the kinship of the two families. Third, to carry on the ancestral line of the husband's family. To give birth to children to carry on the family name was considered a most important responsibility of marriage. Fourth, to preserve a traditional lifestyle together. As long as the two families matched each other socially, and there was a matchmaker to introduce the two, the couple were required to rely on each other and help each other after marriage, whether they love each other or not.

From these we can see that traditional marriage in old China was not based on love. The real purpose was to continue the family tree. The marriage was forced to be accepted and it did not satisfy the needs of the individuals, nor did it result from the attraction between two people. This kind of marriage of Chinese characteristics completely neglected human's spiritual needs and repressed human nature and desire.

However, the progress of the society and the introduction of modern civilization to China have brought new ideas, including science, freedom, equal rights and democracy to Chinese people's minds. Since then, young people have began to look for romance, and to make decisions for their own marriages. Arranged marriages were abolished, and freedom of love and marriage became popular in Chinese society.

The present Chinese family system is quite different from the traditional structure. Big families with four generations living under one roof are seldom seen, and the nuclear family has become the dominant family form, the influence from families is gradually weakened. Men and women now have equal positions at home. Women are becoming more independent, and most of them work to help support the family economically. Love is now a priority in marriage and has become the ethical standard for those deciding to marry.

家庭篇 Family

15. 孩子至上

生育问题在中国家庭中占有很重要的地位。在历史上，子孙满堂被看做一件"有福气"的事情。自从20世纪80年代"计划生育"成为中国的基本国策后，拥有独生子女的家庭越来越多，这令中国人更加珍惜、重视子女。因此，孩子成为家庭的中心也就不足为奇了。

古语曰：不孝有三，无后为大，足见孩子在中国人心中的地位。孩子不但是中国家庭中维系感情的纽带，也是家庭的希望。望子成龙、望女成凤是中国人的普遍心理。为了下一代，中国人往往不惜一切代价。古代有"孟母三迁"的故事，现今的父母为孩子成长也是竭尽全力，学钢琴、请家教、陪孩子读书……只要是力所能及的，父母都在所不惜。

一般情况下，大多数中国父母对儿子的期望更多地表现在事业和权势的层面，而对女儿的期望则更多的是家庭和睦。这个观念仍然沿袭着中国"男主外、女主内"的传统思想。虽然在现代社会里，随着独生子女比例的加大，男女平等的观念越来越深入人心，职业女性也越来越为社会所尊重，但根据调查结果来看，大多数中国人仍保持着男性应该事业有成、女性应该懂得持家的传统观念。

有这样一个关于一棵大树的故事，或许它就是对中国父母生动的反映。

有一个小孩子，在他很小的时候，经常去一棵大树下玩儿。大树非常喜欢这个小孩，常对他说：你每天都过来，让我们一起开心地玩儿吧！于是那个小孩常去大树下玩耍。

许多年过去了，小孩长大了，可是大树还是对他说，孩子，让我们大家一起玩吧！孩子说：不，我现在不想玩了，我想要玩具，你能给我吗？大树说：我没有玩具，我只有果实，你可以把我的果实摘下换成钱去买玩具。孩子很高兴地把果实摘下来换成了玩具。

又是很多年过去了，小孩子长大成人了，有了自己的家庭。这一天他又来到大树下，大树还是对他说：孩子，让我们一起玩儿吧！孩子说：不，我现在有自己的家了，我需要房子，你能帮我吗？大树说：我没有房子，可是你可以把我的树干和树枝砍了，做你建房子的材料。孩子照它说的做了，于是大树就只剩下一个树桩。

家庭篇 Family

就这样，几十年过去了，当初那个孩子也成了一个老人。这一天他又来到大树前。大树对他说：我现在什么也没有了，帮不了你了。老人说：我现在什么都不要了，只想休息一下，你能帮我吗？大树说：那你坐下吧！老人坐在树桩上，好好地休息了一下。

就这样，大树用他的全部帮助了这个孩子，可以说，它为这个孩子付出了一切。

姑且把这个故事变成一首小诗：

有一棵大树，

春天倚着它幻想；

夏天倚着它繁茂；

秋天倚着它成熟；

冬天倚着它沉思。

这棵大树就是父母！

故事中的这颗大树就是中国家庭中父母的真实写照，他们为抚养孩子成人付出了太多的心血，却不求任何回报。

当然，我们知道这种以孩子为中心的做法难免会出现问题。首先，容易造成对子女的溺爱；与溺爱形成强烈对比的就是许多家长对子女的要求过于严格，这种过激的爱源于传统思想——望子成龙、望女成凤的急切心情。这两种做法都值得今天的父母反思。

Child Is Everything

Children are the center of most Chinese families. In the Chinese tradition, a family of many children was considered a blessing. After the implementation of the one-child policy in China, the only child in the family naturally became the key concern of the family.

As the old Chinese saying goes, "Of the three kinds of unfilial acts, the greatest is not to have a son to carry on the family line." Children are considered the most important members in the family, as they are not only the tie that links the whole family together, but also the future hope for the family. Longing to see their children become successful is a common psychological phenomenon among the Chinese people, and there are many Chinese tales about parents making tremendous sacrifices for the good future of their children. In present days, the parents are doing all they can to provide the best environment for the children to grow and learn, accompanying them to various courses, to learn various skills and to invite private teachers to tutor at home, encouraging the children to reach their best potential.

家庭篇 Family

Generally, the expectations of most Chinese parents for their sons involve their potential career, power, influence etc., whereas those of their daughters would be they have a happy and harmonious family in the future. This concept can be viewed as a continuation of the traditional idea in China that "Women should do only housekeeping, leaving the 'outside business' to men". While the concept of gender equality is increasingly taking root in the hearts of people among the growing proportion of the "only child" and career women are also gaining respect of the whole society, survey results indicate that most Chinese still hold the traditional view that males should try to achieve a successful career while females should be good at managing the household.

There is a story about a big tree that is perhaps a vivid reflection of the Chinese parents.

There was once a kid who often played under a big tree. The tree liked the baby very much. It often said to him: "Come to me every day, let's play happily together." Each time the kid agreed and played with it. As years passed by, the kid grew into a child. One day the tree asked him again to play together. The child answered: "I don't want to play with you. I want a toy. Can you give me a toy?" The old tree answered: "I don't have a toy, but I have fruits. You can pick the fruits, sell them to have money and then buy the toys you like." The child followed the tree's advice, picked the fruit and bought the toy.

More years passed, the child grew up and had his own family. One day, he came under the tree again, which said the same words to him: "Let's play together." The man answered: "No, I have a family now, I need a house, can you help me?" The tree answered: "I don't have a house, but you can chop my trunk and branches to build your house." The men chopped the tree, and only the stump of the tree was left.

Several decades later, the men grew into an elder, and came to the tree again. This time, the tree said to him: "I don't have anything left, I can't help you." The old man said: "I don't need anything now. May I just take a rest here?" The old tree said, "OK, sit down here." The old man sat on the stump and had a good rest.

The story perfectly explains the relationship between Chinese parents and children. The parents expend all efforts to raise their children, without asking for anything in return.

家庭篇 Family

16. 养老送终

西方老人以自立为荣,故不服老,也不愿意依赖子女;中国老人则多以有后代照顾为晚年幸福的标志,故希望子女能做到"养老送终"。

孔子曾经说过:"父母在,不远游,游必有方。"意思就是说,如果一个人的父母仍然健在的话,那么他就不应该外出奋斗,如果真的想要外出的话,那么他就必须有一个明确的目标,而且要妥善安排好自己的父母才行。孔子这句话强调的就是中国千百年来传统道德中最根本的一点:孝,即子女应该奉养并孝顺父母。

中国传统社会中强调,个人利益要无条件服从家族利益,以维护家族利益、保持家庭和谐兴旺为目的。在家庭中,注重家长的权威,强调以血缘关系为纽带的人伦辈分关系,这就是中国家族主义精神的集中表现。以"孝"为核心的伦理观念则是对家族精神的一种外化。

"孝"的观念在中国由来已久,源远流长。孔子的学说,就是以"孝"作为仁学之本。中国古代关于孝道的著作《孝经》中则是把"孝"视为天经地义的,强调"孝"

的伦理核心地位和重要价值。

"孝"的基本内容有三个：第一，必须孝敬自己的祖先。为了使血缘关系更加牢固、稳定，"孝"必须要求后人继承祖先的事业，奉行祖先的规矩，恭敬地祭祀祖先。这也是中国人历来都非常重视自己的祖先、喜欢寻根溯源的原因。第二，绝对服从父母的意志，赡养侍奉父母。孔子认为，孝敬父母是做儿女的义务，子女不仅要保证父母在物质生活上的充足，还要让父母生前精神愉悦，不为自己的身后事悬心。这也就是我们常说的，中国人注重的养老送终问题。第三，在做到以上两项以后，要真正做到"孝"，就要求子女要在社会上站稳脚跟，获取自己应有的地位和权力，立业成名，从而能够光宗耀祖，提升家族的荣誉。只有做到这三方面，才算真正实行了孝道。

"养老"，即奉养并孝敬父母，这无疑是中国家庭生活中的一项重要内容。赡养父母作为中国传统孝道的最基本方式，体现着传统的父母与子女的双向养育的功能。千百年来，中国的老百姓自然而然地产生了"养儿防老、积谷防饥"的观念。中国人与西方人不同，个人必须在家庭中有相应的地位进而才能在社会上很好地生活。每个人的一生都必然在家庭中开始，也将在家庭中结束，不可能脱离家庭而单纯地依靠社会存在。因此中国老人的奉养工作历来由子女来承担，而不是像西方社会那样依靠社会保障体系。

由于父系血缘关系传承的缘故，长期以来赡养父母的责任主要是落在男性的肩上，也就说父母年老后大多是和自己的儿子住在一起。女儿负担的责任相对较少。对父母的奉养包括物质上和精神上的奉养。物质上的奉养主要是要满足父母基本的生活需求，还要根据父母的需求为父母提供尽可能好的、有利于其健康的生活环境。精神上的奉养则要在父母的情感上为他们提供慰藉，如发自内心的真诚关心、多花时间陪父母聊天、休闲娱乐等等。这远比物质上的奉养更能让父母感到身心愉悦、健康，从而有利于促进家庭的和睦、社会的稳定。

"送终"，即在父母过世后，子女应尽量为父母办好体面的葬礼，并为父母守丧三年，以显示自己的悲痛之情，体现自己的孝道。不过，今天为父母守丧的做法早已废除了，但是丧葬、祭祀等活动依然存在。每年"清明节"，国人便会带着全家扫墓祭奠，怀念离世亲人。为了发扬这一传统，2008年中国已将"清明节"定为国家的法定节假日。

随着中国"计划生育"政策的普及，独生子女的家庭越来越多，一对夫妻通常要负担双方父母的赡养责任，这使得他们肩上的责任日渐加重。更有甚者，由于独生子女离家外出工作，家庭"空巢"现象大量出现，老年人的生活水平和质量已引起社会的关注。这还有待于国家社会保障体系的逐步完善，从而有效地减轻子女的赡养负担；同时也需要中国老人不断转变固有的传统观念。但是，很长的一段时期内，中国老人的赡养问题依然有赖于儿女来承担。

Filial Piety — Chinese Old Tradition

Unlike aging parents in the West who typically don't like to admit their age and prefer to remain independent, aging Chinese parents are fond of depending on their children. Young people in China are expected to look after their parents when they reach old age, as well as to revere them and sacrifice to them after they die.

Confucius said: "While your parents are alive, you do not travel far. If you have to travel, you must have a stated destination." In Confucian thought, a child must take care of their aging parents when they are still alive and if he really needs to leave them, he must have a clear aim and make good arrangement for the parents. This saying is to emphasize the most fundamental part of Chinese traditional moral value adopted over the thousands of years — the filial piety, to take care of the parents and be obedient to them.

In traditional Chinese society, individual interests should submit to the family interests so that the interests and

harmony of the family can be protected. In a family, the parents are the absolute authorities and all relations are based on the blood bonds. This embodies the Chinese familism system and the externalization of this system is the ethical concept with the core of "filial piety".

"Filial piety" is a custom rooted in ancient Chinese tradition. Although Confucius' concept of humaneness is the ultimate goal of his philosophy, this goal begins with filial piety. The main source of our knowledge regarding the importance of this goal is *The Book of Filial Piety*. In this work, Confucius regards filial piety as an unalterable principle and declares it an ethical core value.

"Filial piety" contains three features. The first is to show filial respect for the ancestors in order to secure a strong and stable blood relationship across generations. Children have to carry on their ancestor's undertakings, pursue their ancestor's customs, and offer sacrifices to their ancestors. Chinese people always care for their ancestors and like to search for things that are related to them. The second feature states that children must obey their parents' will and support them. Confucius thinks that sons and daughters should consider it a moral obligation to look after their parents. They should not only provide sufficient material well-being during their lives, but also make their parents happy so they do not worry for their children after their deaths. This means that the respect a child being normally required to show toward their parents was a duty that extended beyond the death of the parent. Thirdly, in addition to the above, "filial piety" also requires that the sons and daughters achieve good social status, position and power. By gaining status they can make their ancestors illustrious and promote their family's honor. Only when children accomplish these three requirements can they fulfill their "filial piety."

A child providing for their parents embodies a fundamental value in Chinese tradition. It reciprocates the nurturing functions between parents and children. For thousands of years, it has been natural for the Chinese to equate, "having a son to alleviate old age and accumulating grains to alleviate hunger." In contrast to Western belief, every Chinese person depends on the family from birth to death. Thus the aging parents in China are supported by their children rather than the social security system in the West.

These bonds run through the blood linage along relatives on the paternal side creating a patriarchal society with patriarchal behavior, meaning that Chinese parents must be supported and served by their sons rather than their daughters. Due to the resulting relationships and the principles that support it, one of

家庭篇 Family

the moral standards in Chinese society has become the extent to which a child can provide for the parents.

When the parents pass away, the children should offer ritual sacrifices and mourn them for three years. However, the mourning practice has long been abolished. Rituals and sacrifices still exist. On the day of the Qingming Festival (Tomb-sweeping Day) every year, Chinese people go to sweep the tombs of the dead and mourn for them. To promote this tradition, the Chinese government included it a legal holiday in 2008.

Recent social and economic development and government birth control policies have resulted in more and more single child families. The result is that a single young couple often has to be responsible for both sets of parents. Thus, the duty of supporting parents has become very heavy. Moreover, when the single child does not live with their parents or works in another city, old parents will inevitable end up living alone. Although the living conditions and the quality of life issues facing the older generation have aroused public attention, the solution to these problems will take time as the social security system improve over time. Then, parents will not have to depend only on their children for support in their old age. But until a social security system is completely implemented in China, older Chinese parents still have to depend on their children.

德行篇

Moral Principles

17. 勤　勉

许多经常接触中国的外国人都对中国人勤勉的品格有着深刻的体会。许多西方人都承认他们在勤奋刻苦方面不敌中国人。一些外国人到中国后发现，中国人加班十分普遍，留给自己的休闲时间则少之又少。

在中国人的传统中，勤奋不仅是一种励志的精神力量，还具有伦理道德的色彩。中国人信奉"天道酬勤"，认为勤奋符合天理人道的自然规律。传统的中国人讲求"鞠躬尽瘁，死而后已"，笃信"勤能补拙"。

中华民族推崇的人生理想，是追求有所作为；认定的成才之路，便是发奋学习和勤勉工作。中国人重视读书、勤奋好学，这已成为世代相传的优良传统。中国民间有许多关于学习的格言，如："少壮不努力，老大徒伤悲"、"活到老，学到老"等，也流传着很多古人发愤苦读的故事。

中国人对勤劳的赞美在传统神话故事中也常有所反映。中国的神话里常有仙女爱上普通书生或农民的情节，男主人公由于自己的勤劳得到了爱情，从而有了家并过上富足的生活。这个勤劳朴实的男主人公体现的正是中

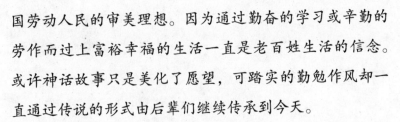
国劳动人民的审美理想。因为通过勤奋的学习或辛勤的劳作而过上富裕幸福的生活一直是老百姓生活的信念。或许神话故事只是美化了愿望，可踏实的勤勉作风却一直通过传说的形式由后辈们继续传承到今天。

中国式的勤劳，就是迎接每一件工作时，都将其视为特别的任务，在完成工作的过程中保持认真的态度，并表现出一种发自内心的迫切感。中国首富李嘉诚的创业故事为不少人所熟悉。李嘉诚年轻时曾在一家塑胶厂当推销员，他深知，要想成为一名成功的推销员，首要的是勤奋。当其他同事每天只工作八小时的时候，李嘉诚就工作十六个小时，天天如此。就这样，李嘉诚只花了一年时间，业绩便超越其他六位同事，成为全厂营业额最高的推销员。他对于"打工"的看法是："对自己的份内工作，我绝对全身心投入，从不仅仅为赚钱糊口，向老板交差了事，而是将之当做自己的事业。"

中国人为什么会这样勤劳呢？中国传统社会是以农业为主的社会，小农经济比重最大。由于土地有限，人们获得财富主要靠日出而作、日落而息的辛苦劳动。在这种经济模式下，勤劳是必然的，否则就会饿肚子。中国古代社会还有一部分人是靠商业获得财富。虽然社会离不开商业，但是，重农轻商的传统思想使商人的社会地位并不高，一夜暴富的大商人往往被人看不起。总的来说，中国传统社会不管是占人口大多数的农民，还是占少数的商人，大都必须一点点地积累财富。可以说，中国人的勤劳是长久以来独特的自然环境和社会环境造成的。

中国改革开放 30 年来，经济有了显著的增长，但毕竟人口多、底子薄，很多中国人仍需要通过勤奋工作来维持生计。但也有相当多的中国人在衣食无忧后仍然向往更富足的生活，做更大的事业，所以还在勤劳地耕耘着。成千上万普普通通的中国人正是凭着那么一股子勤奋工作的劲头，才创造了巨大的财富，也才有了 30 年来国家经济的高速发展。

Diligence

Many Westerners know from their experience of working with the Chinese that they are a hard-working people. In fact, most Westerners would readily admit that they are not as diligent toward their work as the Chinese. In China, most people often work overtime, leaving themselves very little leisure time after work.

Chinese tradition teaches that diligence is not only a

Moral Principles

德行篇

spiritual strength aimed at achievement, but part of the moral principles guiding one's life. The Chinese believe diligence is in conformity with the course of human justice and natural law. Chinese tradition stresses "be loyal and devoted to the last." Diligence in working is also the means by which one makes up for any lack of natural talent.

The Chinese nation bestows high praise to those whose aim in life is to do something worthwhile. They believe that if one is diligent in studying and working, one will be successful. This fine tradition has been passed from generation to generation in such learned sayings as, "One will vainly regret in old age one's laziness in youth" and "Keep learning as long as one is alive."

There are, in addition, many beautiful fairy tale stories throughout Chinese history praising diligence. More often than not the plot has a pretty fairy maiden falling in love with a poor scholar who studies late into the night or a young farmer, who though unrefined and simple, works extremely hard. In these stories, the male characters gain love, satisfy their family and earn richness due to their diligence. These fairy tales express the Chinese people's moral beliefs and aesthetic standards. As common people always believe that hard study and work will lead to a rich and happy life. The fairy tales may just reflect the beautiful wishes, but the habit of deligence has been passed down through legends.

The Chinese style of diligence is illustrated in the fact that everyone treats every job with the same importance as a special assignment that requires them to finish the job as conscientiously as possible. You have probably heard the story of how the richest person in China, Li Ka-shing, started his business empire. When he was young, Li Ka-shing was a salesman in a rubber factory. He was deeply aware of the fact that, if he wanted to be a successful salesman, he had to be diligent. When other people worked only eight hours per day, he would work sixteen hours. This way, in just one year, he rose above the six other salesmen in the company to become the top salesman with the highest earnings. He states that he treats all his work sincerely and as part of his personal cause, not just as work for a boss. He never thinks of his efforts as a job he does just to make a living or to feed his family and himself.

Why have Chinese people been so diligent? A primary reason is that Chinese traditional society is based on an agricultural economy with a large percentage of small farmers. Since there was limited space for farm land, the only way to gather a larger harvest was to work harder and longer, from sunrise to sundown. Under this kind of economic regime, if you don't work hard, you go hungry. Of course, in ancient China, there were also a small segment of people who made a living doing various kinds of business and some of these people became rich. But, traditional Chinese culture held that business was not a good way to make a living because it could not make a society rich. So, these early Chinese businessmen were held in very low esteem. People looked down on those who suddenly earned big money. At any rate, whether one was a farmer or businessman, they all accumulated their wealth little by little in traditional Chinese society. Thus, it is fair to say the quality of diligence of the Chinese comes from a long and unique set of natural and social circumstances.

China has made many reforms during the thirty years it opens to the outside world, yet despite these remarkable economic achievements China has a large population and a poor foundation from which to start. Many Chinese people have to work hard just to make a living. However, there are many ordinary Chinese people, who through their hard work, gained tremendous wealth, hence made the fast development of the national economy during the recent three decades a reality.

18. 务　实

　　有这样一个小故事很是耐人寻味：一个哲学家乘船
过江，他问船夫："你懂哲学吗？"船夫答道："不懂"。
哲学家说："那么，你就失去了一半的生命。"这时，江
上起了风浪，船翻了，两人都掉进了江里。船夫问哲学
家："你会游泳吗？"哲学家答："不会。"船夫说："那
你就失去了全部生命。"故事里的船夫信奉的便是务实的
信念！

　　中国人更愿意面对现实，做实用主义者，尽力过好
每一天，让自己过得平和、舒适和富足。在以农业为生
存根基的中国，农业生产的节奏早已与国民生活的节奏
契合。中国的传统节日，包括最隆重的春节，均来源于
农事，是由农业节气演化而成的，并不像许多其他民族
那样，节日多源于宗教。在这样的文化氛围内，重农思
想的产生便是顺理成章的事情。中国人很早就认识到农
耕是财富的来源。向土地讨生活来不得半点的浮夸和虚
妄。作为华人主体的农民，在日复一日、年复一年的耕
作过程中领悟到一个朴实的道理：利无幸至，力不虚掷，

即说空话大话毫无意义，全心做事才有收获。在此基础上升华衍射，形成了中国人"重实际而黜玄想"的民族性格。务实精神是"一分耕耘，一分收获"的农耕生活导致的一种群体趋向。这种务实作风也感染了世人，"大人不华，君子务实"是中国贤哲们一向倡导的精神。

"实用理性"是儒学乃至整个中国文化心理的一个重要特征。它不是用神秘的、狂热的而是用冷静的、现实的态度来认识和处理事物；不是禁欲或纵欲式地扼杀或放任情感欲望，而是用理智来引导、满足或节制欲望；它对纯思辨的抽象和纯理论的讨论争辩没有兴趣，而是更看重如何在现实生活中妥善处理具体事务。

"重实际而黜玄想"的中华民族性格的另一个重要表现，是中国人对待宗教神鬼的态度。孔子曰："未能事人，焉能事鬼"；"未知生，焉知死"。中国自周秦以后的两千余年间，虽有种种土生的或外来的宗教流传，但基本上没有陷入全民族的宗教迷狂。世俗的、入世的思想始终压倒神异的、出世的思想。中国人不需要外在的、上帝的命令，不盲目服从非理性的权威，却依然自信可以完善自我。就主体而言，中国人的"终极关怀"，即对生命最高意义的追求，不是在"彼岸"世界求解脱，而是在"此岸"世界做圣贤，实现立德、立功、立言。这也正是中国传统文化的主流是入世的儒学而不是出世的宗教的根本原因。

正是这种民族性格使中国人发展了实用的经验理论，而不太注重纯理论的玄思，亚里士多德式的不以实用为目的、而是在好奇心驱使下的探求自然奥秘的文化较少在中国产生。中国人形成的思维定式是注意切实领会，并不追求精密严谨的思辨体系，从而被西方人称为"最善于处理实际事务"的民族。中国人无论遇着什么样的问题，不管大小难易，总是以个人经验、意见、心思、手腕来处理，而不擅长寻求理论上的证据。

务实，即重实效，尤其是立竿见影的。中国人习惯在衡量得失利害之后得到对现实形势的一个判断，即确认实际情况是怎样的，然后根据了解的这个情况，决定自己的行止进退，以求得最佳结果。这就是中国人的"务实"。

在务实精神或者说在"实用理性"的精神支配之下，中国人在各种实务中，包括农、工、商以及政治、学术、人际关系等方面都习惯于深思熟虑，不动声色，冷静慎重，注意实践的可行性和现实的逻辑依据，不冲动，不狂热，重功能，重效果。诚如恩格斯所说，在一切实际事务中，中国人远胜过一切东方民族。正是由于中国农民和士人的务实精神以及由此生发的非宗教的实用理性，使中国创造了辉煌的古代文化，并在封建社会上千年的历史中

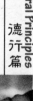

长期处于世界前列。而同时期被神学蒙昧主义所笼罩的
中世纪欧洲各国则相形见绌，难以望其项背。

Pragmatism

There is a short tale that stands careful reading. A philosopher took a ferry across the river. He asked the boatman: "Do you understand philosophy?" The boatman answered: "I don't." The philosopher said: "In that way you have lost half of your life." At this moment, a storm arose and the boat turned over. The boatman asked the philosopher: "Do you know how to swim?" The philosophy answered: "I don't." The boatman said: "In that way you will lose all of your life." The boatman in the tale serves as a realistic representation of Chinese character.

Chinese people are very willing to be realistic and pragmatic. They try their best to spend day to day life in such comfort, peace and happiness as possible. Yet, as China first developed as an agricultural society, the pace of the farmers' life is inextricably joined with their social environment. All of the Chinese traditional holidays, including Spring Festival Days, originated in the activities of farming seasons. This is unlike other nationalities whose holidays are primarily related to their religious beliefs. Coming from this kind of cultural background, it is certainly reasonable that the Chinese would place more stress on agriculture in general. Chinese people realized long ago that farming was the source of income. When your life depends on working the earth, there is no room for exaggeration or speculative beliefs. The farmers, as the majority of the Chinese people, understood a simple truth from their daily and seasonal labor cultivating the earth: there is no free lunch, only your efforts will be repaid. Thus, there was no point in empty talk or boasts, only diligent work could be rewarded. This national characteristic has been distilled from lived experience, "Be devoted to the facts and dismiss illusion," which stems from the fact that "The more one ploughs and weeds, the better the crop." This spirit has become a fundamental disposition of the nation. It also stands as the criteria for a wise and able person, "The excellent are not flashy and the gentlemen are realistic and pragmatic."

This "pragmatism" is an important character of Confucianism and even in Chinese cultural psychology. It does not depend on mysterious and fanatical approaches, but employs a peaceful and realistic approach to the circumstances at hand. It doesn't restrain or indulge sensual passion, but binds itself to reason and provides a guide to meet or control sensual passion. It is not interested in discussions of an abstract or speculative nature or pure theory and only pays attention to the appropriate treatment of the practical 'nuts and bolts' of real life.

Another aspect of this "pragmatism" is an attitude toward the supernatural. Confucius emphasized the world of the living when he said: "While still unable to do your duty to the living, how can you do your duty to the dead?" and moreover, "Not yet understanding life how can you understand death?" Although there have been many kinds of religions that have passed through China in the two thousand years since the Zhou and Qin dynasties, the Chinese nation did not get lost in these various religions. They still believe common social customs prevail over the idea of a mystical belief that stands aloof from worldly pursuits. The Chinese people do not obey orders from God, and they are not overawed by unreasonable authority, but believe in their own competence to improve themselves. In principle, the Chinese people's "ultimate concern" is in pursuit of the highest significance of life by being a sage and man of virtue, establishing morality, being recognized, and achieving glory by writing and passing down the wisdom. This is the mainstream of Chinese traditional culture and stands as the difference between Confucianism and religions that renounce the world.

Due to this influence on their national character, Chinese people exhibit a practical way of thinking about things and do not pay much attention to philosophical theory. Aristotle's stress on seeking the natural world is prompted by curiosity not by a practical goal would not find many adherents in China. The Chinese approach is a practical understanding concerned with results rather than a precise ideological system. The Chinese are often referred to by Westerners as "having a special ability in dealing with practical matters." When Chinese people confront any kind of problem, whether big or small, difficult or easy, they always use personal experience, opinion, ideal and finesse, they never explore theory to solve a problem.

The result of this approach is a concern with immediate results relating to work. Chinese people routinely weigh up the possible gains and losses first as they assess the situation. After understanding the facts, they normally adopt a realistic attitude in order to seize the maximum benefit and at the same time please everybody involved with the situation as well as leave plenty of room for further action if needed.

Moral Principles

德
行
篇

Chinese people are guided by the spirit of this "pragmatic approach" in their considerations in all fields, including agriculture, industry, business, politics, academics and interpersonal relations. They do not allow emotions to change their voice or expression, but deal with things carefully and calmly, paying attention to common sense and logic rather than impulsiveness or passion. This is because their primary concern is with results. Truly, as Frederick Engels once said, the Chinese people have, over all the other oriental nations, an approach to deal with reality. Due to the Chinese farmers and scholars' spirit of being "devoted to facts" and having "a pragmatic approach," China created a dazzling ancient culture leading the world and lasting for over a thousand years during the feudal society. Yet the European countries of that time were lost in theological obscurantism and thus failed to secure a leading place in the world.

19. 人无信不立

"言必信，行必果"，"一言既出，驷马难追"……这些流传了千百年的古语，都形象地表达了中华民族诚实守信的品质。在中国几千年的文明史中，人们不但为诚实守信的美德大唱颂歌，而且努力地身体力行。

诚实守信、信守诺言是中国人为人处事的一种美德，更是中国人的处世之本。所谓诚实，就是忠诚老实，不讲假话。诚实的人能忠实于事物的本来面目，不歪曲，不篡改事实，光明磊落，言语真切，处事实在。诚实的人反对投机取巧，趋炎附势，见风使舵，争功推过，弄虚作假，口是心非。

中国是文明古国、礼仪之邦，历来重视诚实守信的道德修养。东汉许慎在《说文解字》中说："信，诚也"。古代的圣贤哲人对诚信有诸多阐述。孔子多次讲过诚信，如"信则人任焉"；"自古皆有死，民无信不立。"孟子论诚信："至诚而不动者，未之有也；不诚，未有能动者也。"荀子认为"养心莫善于诚"。墨子也极讲诚信："志不强者智不达，言不信者行不果。"老子把诚信作为人生行为

德行篇

的重要准则："轻诺必寡信，多易必多难。"庄子也极重诚信："真者，精诚之至也。不精不诚，不能动人。"这就把诚信提高到一个新的境界。韩非子则认为"巧诈不如拙诚。"总之，古代的圣贤哲人把诚信作为一项崇高的美德加以颂扬。

一个人要想在社会立足，干出一番事业，就必须具有诚实守信的品德。一个弄虚作假、欺上瞒下、糊弄国家与社会，骗取荣誉与报酬的人，是要遭人唾骂的。诚实守信首先是一种社会公德，是社会对做人的基本要求。

中国古代也有不讲诚信而自食恶果的例证——烽火戏诸侯。西周建都镐（今长安县），接近戎人。周天子与诸侯相约，要是戎人来犯就点燃烽火、击鼓报警，请诸侯来救。周幽王的爱妃不爱笑，唯独看到烽火燃起，诸侯的军队慌慌张张从四面赶来时才大笑不止。周幽王为博得爱妃高兴，数次无故燃起烽火，诸侯的军队多次赶到而不见戎人，很是气愤。后来戎人真的来了，当烽火再燃起时，已无人来救。最终周幽王被杀于骊山之下，为天下人所耻笑。

朱熹说，人与人要"合义则言，不合义则不言。言义，则其言必可践而行之矣！"这就是说"轻诺寡信则殆"。对于成大事的人而言，手中都有一张"信用卡"——以诚信处世。诚信，不仅是做人的准则，也是处世的原则和方法。为人处世以"信"为原则，讲信义、重信义，这样的人才会为世人所接受，才会在危难之时获得帮助。

三国时代的诸葛亮四出祁山时，所率兵马只有十多万人，而司马懿却有精兵30万。正当蜀、魏在祁山对阵的紧急时刻，蜀军有1万人因服役期满，需退役回乡。而离去1万人，会大大影响蜀军的战斗力。服役期满的士兵也忧心忡忡：大战在即，回乡的愿望恐怕要化为泡影。这时，军中很多将士向诸葛建议：延期服役一个月，待大战结束后再让老兵们还乡。诸葛亮断然地说："治国治军必须以信为本。老兵们归心似箭，家中父母妻儿望眼欲穿，我怎能因一时需要而失信于民呢？"说完，诸葛亮下令各部，让服役期满的老兵速速返乡。诸葛亮的命令一下，老兵们几乎不敢相信自己的耳朵，随后一个个热泪盈眶，激动不已，决定不走了。"丞相待我们恩重如山，如今正是用人之际，我们要奋勇杀敌，报答丞相！"老兵们的激情对在役的士兵则是莫大的鼓励。蜀军上下群情激愤，士气高昂，在形势不利的情况下击败了魏军。诸葛亮以信带兵取得了以少胜多的战绩。

人无信不立，良好的信誉会给自己的行动带来意想不到的便利。诚实、守信也是形成强大亲和力的基础。诚实守信的人会使人产生与之交往的愿望，在某种程度上，还可以消除不利因素带来的障碍，使困境变为坦途。

中国人的诚信观念在近些年来经济快速发展情况下被一些利欲熏心、急功近利的人抛在了脑后。也许他们能求得暂时的利益，但不会长久。中国人依然坚信"人无信不立"的信条，更希望能传给子孙后代，让他们继承和发扬这一美德。

A Man Stands by His Word

"Keep to your word, be resolute in deed" and "Even four horses cannot take back what you have said" are old sayings circulated among Chinese people for thousands of years. They all express the Chinese character regarding honesty and trustworthiness. Over the thousands of years of Chinese civilization, Chinese people not only praised the traditional virtues of sincerity and faithfulness, but carried them out in their every effort.

Keeping a promise is a virtue to Chinese people who know how to conduct themselves and deal with their affairs. It is also Chinese people's way of dealing with the world. By honesty, we mean being truthful and straightforward. An honest person must be faithful to the facts, do not distort or modify facts, at the same time, do not hide one's true opinion, be frank and forthright, speak clearly. An honest person does not support people who are opportunists and often fawn upon the rich and powerful, trim their sail to the wind, crave greatness and success but shift the responsibility on to others, or employ trickery or deception.

As an ancient civilization, China has always advocated proper manners, and always valued ethical training for the virtues of honesty and faithfulness. Xu Shen (58 -147) of the Eastern Han Dynasty, the author of *Shuowen Jiezi*, the first etymological Chinese character dictionary, explained it this simple way: "True is honest." Ancient oracle philosophers had many elaborate sayings about good faith. Confucius spoke about good faith many times, for example, "He who is of good faith is trusted by the people," "From ancient times, death has been the lot of men, but a people without faith cannot stand." Mencius also discussed this when he wrote that, "Never has there been one possessed of complete sincerity, and did not move others. Never has there been one who had not sincerity and was able to move others." Xun Zi, a Confucian philosopher (313-238 BC) declared that, "The good conduct of a nourishing heart is sincerity." Mo Zi, another philosopher who lived during the Hundred Schools of Thought Period (468-376 BC) also stressed sincerity:

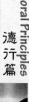

"One's wisdom will not be far-reaching whose purpose is not firm. One's action will not be effective whose promises are not kept." Lao Zi, a philosopher of ancient China in the 6th century BC and a central figure in Taoism, regarded sincerity as an important guiding principle of human behavior and said: "Who finds it easy to promise finds it hard to be trusted, who takes things lightly finds things difficult." Zhuang Zi, another influential philosopher who lived around the 4th century BC, also placed a high value upon sincerity and said: "By the 'truth' I mean purity and sincerity in their highest degrees. He who lacks purity and sincerity cannot move others." His teachings on this subject brought the philosophy of sincerity to a higher level. As the philosopher Han Feizi (280-233 BC) wrote: "Even the cleverest trick is no match for the power of dull sincerity." Thus, ancient sages and men of virtue praised sincerity and trust as a sign of moral excellence.

If people want to establish themselves in society and seek official advancement, they must possess the moral character of sincerity and must keep their promises. The fate of those who use trickery, conceal the true state of affairs from people both above and below, fool the country and society, and seek honors and reward through fraud and deception, is to be spit on and cursed by all people. Sincerity and keeping one's promises are the first characteristics of a social ethics and Chinese society's most basic request of the people.

There are famous stories about people who have fallen victim to their own evil deeds by their insincerity and lies. The Western Zhou Dynasty (1046-771 BC) founded its capital at Hao (near the present-day Chang'an County in Shaanxi Province), which was close to an ancient ethnic group called the Rong (a minority tribe) in the west. King You (reigned 781-771 BC) set up a system of warning beacons in times of extreme danger. Once the Rong invaded the border, the beacon towers were made to smoke and the armies were gathered. The story goes that the concubine of the King You seldom smiled, but she laughed when seeing armies gathered in a rush. To please her, King You often ordered to light the beacons. The armies saw the signals from the beacons and rode at full speed to the capital to assist the King and only to learn angrily that the King did this simply to make his concubine smile. Later, the Rong staged an armed rebellion against the Western Zhou Dynasty. King You urgently ordered the beacon towers to be lit, but tired of the false alarms all the armies stayed where they were. Consequently, King You was killed at the foot of Mt. Lishan and laughed at by all. From

Moral Principles

德行篇

this story comes the Chinese idiom: "The sovereign rulers are fooled by the beacon fire."

Zhu Xi, a Confucian scholar of the Song Dynasty (960-1279), said allies should, "cling to the same principle and discuss that, if not, they shouldn't converse." What this means is that if one takes a promise lightly and fails to keep his word, he will put himself in a dangerous position. If people want to accomplish anything in life they have to maintain a good reputation, and to do this they must keep their word. Sincerity and keeping one's promise is not only a moral principal, but also a philosophy of life, a way of conducting oneself in society. Maintaining good values and acting in good faith lead to the kind of person that will win people's confidence and their assistance when needed.

Zhuge Liang (181–234) was the Prime Minister for Shu Han during the Three Kingdoms Period. When Zhuge Liang attacked Qishan for the fourth time, he had only ten-thousand troops against the thirty-thousand troops of Sima Yi. As the two armies held their positions on the battle front, there were ten-thousand Shu soldiers who had completed their term of service and should be allowed to retire. But if these ten-thousand soldiers left at this critical time, it would largely deplete the capacity of the Shu army to fight. Understandably, these soldiers were anxious and afraid to extend their service in the face of a battle with a much larger enemy. His officers urged Zhuge Liang to extend these soldiers' service by one month, and promise them they could retire after the battle. Zhuge Liang, however, categorically rejected this and said: "The foundation for ruling a country and commanding troops is keeping your word. Old soldiers long to return home and their families are anxiously waiting for them. How can I break my promise and jeopardize their confidence in me?" He then gave the order allowing all the old soldiers to return to their homes immediately. The old soldiers cried tears of happiness, but they then decided not to go back to home immediately. They realized that, in honoring his word, the Prime Minister had made a profound decision that held grim consequences for their country and decided that they would fight the enemy bravely to repay him for keeping his word. This decision by the old soldiers lifted the spirits of all the soldiers, encouraging the entire army. Thus, the Shu army quickly defeated the Wei army. Being true to his word with his soldiers, Zhuge Liang was able to lead his small army in the defeat of a much larger enemy.

A man who stands by his word will experience an even greater gain than by his actual deeds. Sincerity and keep-

Moral Principles

德行篇

144

ing one's promise is also the foundation for the formation of a natural identification or affinity. People are attracted to individuals who are honest and trustworthy. To some extent, these qualities can also clear away destructive obstacles and straighten out difficult situations. Nonetheless, with the fast growing economy in recent years, these qualities are largely being ignored by some people who are blinded by greed, seeking instant success and quick benefits. They may gain certain interest for the time being, but it won't last long. The Chinese still hold the belief that "A man should stand by his word." And they hope to pass that to their descendants to carry this virtue forward.

20. "随便"与"内圆外方"

　　中国人嘴巴上常常喜欢说："随便，你看着办！"有客人到家里来做客，主人问客人，喝什么？茶、咖啡还是果汁？客人常说，随便，什么都行。这其实不是无所谓，而是让你看着办，不经意间可以看出自己在主人眼里的地位。又如，下属请示领导事情怎么办？领导说，"你看着办吧"。这说明领导对你的信任。如果事情办得好，领导会加倍赏识；如果没办好，下属的能力会在领导心中打一定折扣。可见"随便"里面潜藏着很多学问。

　　"随便"，正是孔子"无可无不可"哲学的体现。儒家谈"经权"，要我们"执两用中"，在不断变动的环境中，"持经达权"。每个人都处在变化中，时时有不同的情况，我们如果不加考虑，马上凭自己的意愿，说出个人的意见，万一对方觉得为难，非但"不敬"，简直就有"不仁"的可能。不如将心比心，先说"随便"，好让彼此有个商量。"随便"绝不是"马马虎虎"。我们将心比心，既不希望人家"马马虎虎"待我，也不可以"马马虎虎"待人。孔子希望我们断绝四种毛病：不主观猜测、不独断偏激、不固执已见、也不自私自利。要绝此四项，即该"随便"才随便，不该"随便"绝不可以随便。这也体现了中国人的处世原则——内方外圆。它并不是老于世故、老谋深算者的处世哲学。这其中，"内方"，表明了对自己理想、原则和信念的坚持，而"外圆"，则表现为与周围环境融洽协调，以减少阻力和矛盾。

中国古代名著《周髀算经》里有言："方属地，圆属天，天圆地方"。古代曾以圆方作为天地的代称，寓意为在不断追求完美的过程中，永葆恒久的生命力。"圆"，是中国道家通变与趋时的学问。而"方"，是中国儒家人格修养的理想境界。可以说，圆方互容，儒道互补，构成了中国传统文化的主体精神。"方"，乃为人之本；"圆"，乃处世之道。方在圆中，圆融于方，两者相互交融。总之，合理运用"方圆"之道，就能无往不胜，所向披靡，无论是趋进，还是退止，都能泰然自若。圆并不是指做人奸猾，而是一种圆通，宽厚融通，与人为善。圆的压力最小，圆的张力最大，圆的可塑性最强。中国人正是充分利用了圆的这些特性，把它作为自己的处事锦囊、处事原则，以不变应万变，开发出无尽的生命力和创造力，开发出无限精彩的新天地。

"方"并不是指做人呆板，而是遵循规矩，遵循法则。中国人因悠久的历史积淀而更能深刻体味"没有规矩不能成方圆"、"有所不为才能有所作为"的道理。所以中国人又能够以不变应万变，能够充分认识：人不可以有傲气，但必须有傲骨；人活在天地间必须挺起做人的脊梁。中国人才能做到"富贵不能淫，威武不能屈，贫贱不能移"。也许正是这种信念让中国成为四大文明古国中唯一一个存在至今的国家。

这种外圆内方的事例，在中国历史上早已有之。《三国演义》中有一段"曹操煮酒论英雄"的故事。当时刘备落难投靠曹操，曹操很真诚地接待了刘备。刘备住在许都，在衣带诏签名后，为防曹操谋害，他就在后园种菜，亲自浇灌，以此迷惑曹操，让他放松对自己的戒备。一日，曹操约刘备入府饮酒，议起谁为世之英雄。刘备点遍袁术、袁绍、刘表、孙策、张绣、张鲁，均被曹操一一贬低。曹操指出英雄的标准——"胸怀大志，腹有良谋，有包藏宇宙之机、吞吐天地之志。"刘备问："谁人当之？"曹操说："天下英雄惟使君与我。"刘备本以韬晦之计栖身许都，被曹操点破是英雄后，竟吓得把筷子丢落在地上。恰好当时大雨将至，雷声大作。曹操问刘备为什么把筷子弄掉了，刘备从容俯拾筷子，并说："一震之威，乃至于此。"曹操说："雷乃天地阴阳击搏之声，何为惊怕？"刘备说："我从小害怕雷声，一听见雷声只恨无处躲藏。"自此曹操认为刘备胸无大志，必不能成气候，也就未把他放在心上。刘备巧妙地将自己的慌乱掩饰过去，从而也避免了一场劫难。刘备在煮酒论英雄的对答中是非常聪明的，他用的就是方圆之术。在曹操的哈哈大笑之中，刘备免除了曹操对他的怀疑和嫉忌，最后如愿以偿地逃脱了虎狼之地。至于三国后期的司马懿，更是个外圆内方的高手。他伴装成快要死的人，瞒过了大将军曹爽，达到了保护自己、等待时机的目的，最后实现了自己的抱负，统一了天下。这正是"鹰立似睡，虎行似病"。

总之，人生在世，运用好"方圆"之理，必能无往不胜，所向披靡。以不"随便"的态度来随便，才能执两用中，权变得宜。我们一方面不可以随便说"随便"，一方面也不能够随便理会或处置别人的"随便"。一个有修养、有分寸的中国人，是不随便说"随便"的。

"As You Wish" and "A Combination of External Flexibility and Internal Integrit "

A phrase often on the Chinese lips is, "As you wish." When there is a visiting guest at home, a host asks, "What would you like to drink: tea, coffee or something else?" The guest may answer, "As you wish." This does not mean the guest would not mind what you serve. It inadvertently shows his weight in the eyes of the host. For another instance, you may ask your superior how to deal with a matter. Your superior says, "As you wish." This shows the superior has full confidence in you. If everything worked out fine, the superior would appreciate more of your abilities. If anything went wrong, the appraisal of your abilities would fall in the eyes of your superior. Thus, it can be concluded that there is a lot of knowledge behind "As you wish."

By such a phrase, we mean what Confucian philosophy advocates — "Anything will do." The Confucian ideas suggest that we be adaptable under different situations. People are changing and situations vary. If we speak out our mind without much thought, it may not be respectful or benevolent when others are in an embarrassing situation. We may as well say "As you wish" first to allow for some alternatives. "As you wish" means no "carelessness." We hope neither to be treated carelessly nor to do so to others. Confucius expects us to rid ourselves of four types of problems: wild guesses, arbitrariness, stubbornness and selfishness. To smooth them away, we may use "As you wish" when called for, and never use it when it is not. This also reflects a Chinese way of dealing with things — a good combination of inner integrity and

Moral Principles

德行篇

external flexibility. It is not a sophisticated way of handling people or things. The inner integrity shows one's adherence to principles, ideas, and beliefs, while the external flexibility displays one's adaptation to the outside world, aiming to remove obstacles and conflicts as much as possible.

Zhou Bi Suan Jing, an ancient Chinese work of mathematics and astrology, mentions, square belongs to earth, and circle to heaven, that is, round heaven and square earth. Ancients used circle and square for heaven and earth, symbolizing a constant pursuit for a perfect and everlasting life force. "Circle" is a body of knowledge for the Taoists to achieve change and adapt to the times, while "square" refers to Confucian ideal for characterization. We may conclude that square and circle as well as Confucianism and Taoism form the mainstay of traditional Chinese culture. "Square or integrity" is central to humans; "circle or flexibility" is fundamental to everyday life. They are closely connected. In a word, people can be invincible in dealing with social issues if they use well the square-circle principle. They may remain calm whether going forward or retreating. Circle does not mean cunningness, but a kind of flexibility, being kind and generous to others. Circle has the strongest elasticity, with the least pressure yet largest tension. The Chinese adopt the circle's characteristics as their principles to develop strong adaptation, thus exploring inexhaustible vitality and numerous splendid worlds.

Square does not mean being rigid, but rather following rules or laws. Over many years, the Chinese have gained a better understanding of such principles as "Square or circle cannot be made without rules," and "Those who can refrain from doing anything may have the potential for achievement." The Chinese can use lack of change as the base for coping with various changes, and are aware that he who must not have arrogance must have unyielding bones and that he who lives between heaven and earth must have an unbending back. Only so can the Chinese do the following: never indulge in debauchery because of becoming rich or noble; never yield because of being coerced or suppressed; never stoop low because of being poor or humble. Perhaps, it is such beliefs that make China, one of the four ancient countries with a long history of civilization, the only country to have survived to this day.

Such examples of square-circle have long existed in Chinese history. In a story from *Romance of the Three Kingdoms*, titled "Cao Cao Warms Wine and Rates the Heroes of the Realm", Liu Bei fled to join Cao Cao, the

Moral Principles
德行篇

former meeting the latter's warm reception. When Liu stayed in Xudu, he signed a silk scroll, preparing to rebel against Cao. To avoid Cao's suspicions, Liu took to his back garden, planting and watering vegetables himself. One day, Liu was invited by Cao to drink wine. They talked about who should be considered the heroes of the time. Liu suggested Yuan Shu, Yuan Shao, Liu Biao, Zhang Xiu and Zhang Lu, but none of them were heroes in the eyes of Cao Cao, who then gave the definition of a hero: "a determination to conquer, a mind of marvelous schemes, an ability to encompass the realm, and the will to make it his." "Who merits such a description?" Liu asked. "The heroes of the present day number but two — you, my lord and myself." Cao said. Liu wanted to hide his ambition by temporarily entering into Cao's service in Xudu. When he was caught off guard by Cao calling him a hero, Liu gulped in panic, with his chopsticks slipping to the ground. Then the storm came. A peal of thunder gave him the chance to bend down casually and retrieve them. "See what a clap of thunder has made me do?" he remarked. Cao said, "Thunder is the hitting sound between heaven and earth. Why fear it?" Liu answered, "I have been afraid of thunder since I was young. When hearing thunder, I wish to hide myself." Since then, Cao thought Liu had no ambition and would not become a threat, putting his mind at ease. Liu adroitly concealed his fear, thus avoiding a catastrophe.

In that scenario, Liu Bei was very intelligent. It is the square-circle principle that works. Among Cao's laughter, Liu rid himself of Cao's suspicions and jealousy, and eventually escaped from Cao's control.

Another similar example is Sima Yi. He made General Cao Shuang believe he was nearly on the verge of death to protect his life and wait for his chance. He finally realized his ambition of encompassing the country. This is why hawks stand as if sleeping and tigers walk as if being sick, both pretending to be weak when preying.

In a word, people can be invincible in dealing with social issues if they skillfully use the square-circle principle. With a seemingly casual manner, one can become flexible and adapt to changes. We can neither casually say "As you wish" on the one hand, nor casually interpret it. A refined Chinese with a sense of propriety will never say that in a casual manner.

21. 含蓄的中国人

中国人在表达个人观点时喜欢含蓄。而在很多外国人眼中来看，中国人的这种表达方式令他们费解。当说"好"时不说"好"，却说"还行"、"凑合"、"你以为如何"；当说"不好"时不说"不好"，却总说"再想想"、"不太好"的话。更有趣的是，一个人如果直来直去地说出自己观点的话，则会被认为"没有城府"，属于"直肠子"，是被认为要吃亏的。

中国人言谈举止的含蓄风格可谓源远流长。中华文明博大悠久，早在春秋战国时期，就形成了比较成熟的以"礼"和"仁"为核心的儒家文化。它一方面要求统治者以"德"治天下，另一方面要求百姓严格遵守道德教化，以"修身"为做人之根本。谦虚谨慎、道德崇高的人受到广泛尊重。这种道德规范随着历史的发展渗透到社会大众生活的各个细枝末节，并经历代文人墨客、思想家的维护和社会价值规范的强化而不断地得到巩固。大多数国人都认为，为人处世应该谦逊而含蓄。于是中国人一直以"礼"规范约束自己的言谈举止和人际交往，用现在通俗的话语表达，就是低调，不张扬。于是乎，人与人之间不太善于、也不太愿意直白地表达自己的内心思想和情感。

中国人的这种文化传承在人际交往中明显具有有益的方面。一方面，高看别人，尊重对方，将自己放在一个谦卑的位置容易与人沟通；另一方面，在不晓得对方见解的情况下，可以避免意见冲突，让双方尴尬。

中国人说话，有点像京剧舞台上的演员，本来三两步就可以直达目的，却偏要甩着水袖，踩着莲花步，锵锵锵锵地绕个大圈子。这其实归到了最重要的一点：崇尚儒家伦理的中国人，只有做一个低调而含蓄的人，才符合传统规范。中国人凡事都讲情面，把脸面看得很重要。自己重视面子当然也要给别人充足的面子，因此中国人总喜欢把话说得婉转含蓄，生怕给别人造成难堪。说某一个人胖，用在男人身上叫"富态"，用在女人身上叫"丰满"。过去把强制性地降低体重叫"减肥"，也许是一个"肥"字太惹眼了，于是现在统统都说"瘦身"了。

中国人对含蓄的喜爱和追求使得汉语里产生了大量的成语和比喻，给汉语增加了无穷的魅力。在描述一件事情时，用只有几个字的成语来描述，不但使语言简练，还可以令人回想起这个成语背后悠远的故事，大大丰富了语言的内涵。像描述姑娘漂亮，常用"倾国倾城"，或"沉鱼落雁，闭月羞花"来形容。这姑娘到底有多美？您只要想想，连月亮和花儿都自惭形秽，那可有多美啊！这比又是描写眉毛又是描写鼻子和腰身的大段文字更生动，更简洁，且给读者留下了想象的空间。

俗话说，"逢人只说三分话。"为什么还有七分话不说呢？你也许认为大丈夫光明磊落，应当坦诚相见，事无不可对人言，何必只说三分话呢？其实不然，人与人之间达到以诚相见的境界势必要有一个过程。在这个过程的每个不同阶段，需要运用各种恰如其分的交际方法，方能保证这个过程的顺利完成。含蓄表达也是一种良好的交往方式。

所谓"话到嘴边留半句"即采取恰当的方式、用巧妙的语言对别人的请求做出间接的、含蓄的、灵活的表态。其特点就是不直截了当地表示态度，避免与对方短兵相接式的交锋。这样可以给自己留有回旋的余地。有些问题一时尚不明朗，需要了解事实真相，或看看事态的发展及周围形势的变化，方可拿主张。含蓄表态就能给自己留下一个仔细考虑、慎重决策的余地。否则，"君子一言，驷马难追"，说错话不仅影响自己的威信和声誉，也会因此对人际关系造成不应有的损失。还有就是给对方留一点希望之光，有利于稳定对方的情绪。要求你解决或答复问题的人，内心总是寄予着厚望的，希望事情能如愿以偿，圆满解决。如果突然遭到生硬的拒绝，由于缺乏必要的心理准备，他很可能因过分失望或悲伤，心理上难以平衡，情绪难以稳定，产生偏激言行，有碍于人际交往。

同时，倘若话未完全说死，则使对方感到事情并非毫无希望，也许经过更多的努力或者过一段时间，机会降临，事情会向好的方向转化。然而我们并不是说，任何时候说话都要留半句。事情的发展变化都得有个过程，有时甚至是一个相当长的演变过程。当事情处于发展变化初期，实质性的问题尚未表露出来，还难于断定其好坏、美丑、利弊、胜负之时，就需要等待、观察、了解、研究，切不可以贸然行事，信口开河。

有些经验丰富的人遇到这类问题，会说几句幽默话语，如引用一则寓言故事或一则笑话，而不做直接回答，留给对方去思考、寻味。这可以说是"话到嘴边留半句"含蓄式表达的高招了。

Reserved and Implicit Chinese People

The Chinese are prone to be reserved when expressing personal views, which is often difficult for foreigners to understand. Instead of saying something is good, they may say "not bad", "just so-so", or "How do you like it?". Instead of saying something is not good, they may say "think it over" or "not too good". More interestingly, if a Chinese person is very straightforward with his views, he will be regarded as unsophisticated, or with a simple mind, and is sure to be taken advantage of.

The reserved style of speech and behavior of the Chinese can be traced back long into history. Chinese civilization has a long history and Confucianism, centered on courteousness and benevolence, came into maturity as early as in the Spring Autumn and Warring States Period. On the one hand, it requested that those in power rule the country with their virtues. On the other hand, it requested that the ruled abide by social morality, and "to improve one's self" was the very essence of being a member of the society. Modest and careful people with high moral standard were highly respected. Throughout history, Confucianism has penetrated into all aspects of the life of Chinese people, and been strengthened as norms of social value by generations of educated people and philosophers. The large majority of Chinese people believe that one should keep a low-key and be reserved when socializing with other people.

Thus Chinese people would always follow certain rules of "courteousness" that guide their behaviors and maintain a low-key attitude. As a result, they are not good at or not willing to express themselves or show their emotions in a very frank and straight-forward way.

Such a cultural preference actually benefits interpersonal exchanges. On the one hand, Chinese people regard others highly and respect others, and position themselves humbly to make it easier to communicate with others. One the other hand, when they are not sure about the views of other people, they avoid embarrassment on both sides by not bluntly expressing their views.

When a Chinese speaks of something, he might do it as if performing Peking Opera. The player will always swing the long flowing silk inner sleeves and walk a few steps particular to Peking Opera on the stage for a while before anything is uttered. This is the result of traditional norms of socializing, which follow Confucianism ethics. The Chinese always have considerations for others' feelings, and are concerned with face-saving, not only for themselves but also for others. In terms of speaking of anything, they are tactful and indirect in order not to embarrass anybody. For example, someone who is fat is not always referred to as "fat", but "fortunate-looking" for a male, and "well-shaped" for a female. To avoid saying "losing weight", "keeping in good shape" is used instead.

The tactfulness of the Chinese has resulted in a large number of idioms and metaphors, which add to the rich glamor of the Chinese language. A few characters of an idiom may vividly depict one certain thing in a terse manner, and moreover, there may be a legend behind the idiom, for a richer connotation of the language. When praising the beauty of a young lady, you can use idioms such as "lovely enough to cause the fall of a city or a state", "the beauty overshadows the moon and flowers." How extremely beautiful the girl might be if her appearance lets the beautiful moon and flowers have a sense of inferiority or inadequacy, if her beauty is worth the cost of losing a country? Such praise is much more effective than a wordy description of how she looks, and meanwhile leaves some space for imagination.

As one saying goes, "Never speak to the fullest extent." Why not be straight-forward with one's mind? Should not a gentleman be open and frank? Should a gentleman hold back his true ideas? Though the Chinese believe that interacting with others should result in a frank exchange of views, the frankness will take some time to come. During the process, different and appropriate approaches shall be applied, to the end of a smooth process. Tactfulness serves well in interpersonal exchanges.

"To reserve half of what you want to say to yourself", if applied in an appropriate and tactful way, is one of the approaches to respond to another's request. One's attitude is not straightforwardly shown, avoiding face to face conflict and leaving oneself some room to maneuver. When the truth of a certain matter is not yet clear and needs to be further explored, or figured out how it will develop, or see how the circumstances evolve, it is better to wait before any decision is made. To show one's attitude in a reserved way will certainly leave oneself with some room to think twice and decide in a cautious manner. Once something is said, it can never be taken back again. When improperly said, the words not only have a negative impact on one's reputation, but also do harm to communications with the other party. Besides, by tactfully responding to the party who raised questions or requests, one will leave certain hope and help calm down the emotions of the party. If the party is to be straightforwardly refused, it may not be easy for him to accept the reality. He may show his pessimistic or sad feelings, or become emotionally imbalanced. At that moment, his words and

Moral Principles

德行篇

behaviors are prone to go to extreme, which hinders effective interpersonal communications.

In addition, by one's not being fully outspoken, the other party may feel it is still hopeful to have something accomplished, given time or more effort. Yet that doesn't mean one should always do so. The evolvement of things may take a long time and during the process when the essentials are not yet clarified, it is impossible to tell the situation and make judgment. What is needed is not blunt behavior and irresponsible decision, but rather more observation and careful consideration.

When facing difficult situations and needing to be responsive, an experienced person will respond with a few humorous words, tell a joke or a fable, instead of giving a direct answer. He will leave much room for the other party to think things over. This tactic is a good approach of "reserving half of what you want to say to yourself."

作者简介

　　李钢，哲学博士，北京邮电大学教授，博士生导师，主要从事中西文化比较和社会哲学研究。曾留学英国剑桥大学，并任剑桥中国论坛主席，剑桥中国学生学者联合会副秘书长。近几年主持完成国家级和省部级科研课题七项，在国内外知名学术刊物上发表中英文学术论文七十多篇，出版有《经济哲学论纲》、《社会转型代价论》和《网络文化》等学术著作六部。

Li Gang, Doctor of Philosophy, Doctoral Tutor, is a professor of Beijing University of Posts and Telecommunications. He mainly researches in the Comparative Study of Eastern and Western Cultures and Social Philosophy. During his study at Cambridge University in England, he was the Chairperson of Cambridge China Forum and Vice Secretary-General of the Chinese Students and Scholars Association. In recent years he directed and completed seven national, provincial research projects, and published more than 70 theses on well-known academic journals of China and abroad in either Chinese or English. The six academic works he published include On Economic Philosophy, On the Price of Social Transformation and Network Culture and etc.

责任编辑：翟淑蓉
英文编辑：韩芙芸
封面设计：古　手
印刷监制：佟汉冬

图书在版编目（CIP）数据

中国人的生活哲学：汉英对照 / 李钢编著. —北京：华语教学出版社，2009

ISBN 978-7-80200-411-5

Ⅰ.中…　Ⅱ.李…　Ⅲ.人生哲学—中国—通俗读物—汉、英

Ⅳ.B821-49

中国版本图书馆CIP数据核字（2008）第168726号

中国人的生活哲学

李钢　编著

*

© 华语教学出版社
华语教学出版社出版
（中国北京百万庄大街24号　邮政编码100037）
电话: (86)10-68320585
传真: (86)10-68326333
网址: www.sinolingua.com.cn
电子信箱: hyjx@sinolingua.com.cn
北京外文印刷厂印刷
2009年(16开)第一版
2010年第一版第二次印刷
（汉英）
ISBN 978-7-80200-411-5
定价: 39.00元